Cowboy Dad

Cowboy Dad

Love, Alcoholism, and a Dying Way of Life

MELISSA BROUGHTON

ISBN: 1511901497
ISBN 13: 9781511901499
Library of Congress Control Number: 2015907520
CreateSpace Independent Publishing Platform
North Charleston, South Carolina

Dedication

This book is dedicated to my little brother, R.J., and my mom, Rhonda.

Table of Contents

One

There he stood in the Santa Barbara bus station—a cowboy with scuffed boots, dingy Levis, and a faded jean jacket that whispered desperation; his white handkerchief peeked out of the pocket with a missing button. His scruff and crow's feet framed his handsome face, and a brave mustache seemed to hold him up, keep him from collapsing. In one hand he held a duffle bag full of a couple of flannel shirts, a pair of Wranglers, and Old Spice Deodorant. I knew what was in the bag because I had packed it for him just the day before. His other hand was relaxed, just his thumb tucked into the front pocket of his jeans, trying to convey a strong cowboy stance; I knew better though—he was hanging on for dear life. His cowboy spirit, like his cowboy hat, had a sturdy presence despite all the years of wear and tear.

A buzz of travelers surrounded him and yet they were all a blur— I only saw him, my dad, the Cowboy. I walked toward him with a broken heart that spoke years of disappointment.

"Don't say a word," I said clinching my jaw, biting down my anger.

"Ok," the Cowboy said in a quick, low tone.

I sensed his nervousness, and I wanted answers. "I need to know, why? Why couldn't you do this?"

I held his gaze.

My heart was pleading with every beat, *please explain to me why you are leaving me.*

The Cowboy offered, "I just couldn't, Hun. I can't stay *there*—it's not where I belong." He touched his hat, looked away.

"There" was the Santa Barbara Rescue Mission Recovery Center where I had taken him just the day before, hoping that it would be the answer when all else failed. I should have known better, but I was stubbornly hopeful, like a calf escaping out of a shoot—sensing freedom—only to be roped in by the cowboy wanting a rodeo win.

And then I spoke the last words my Dad would ever hear me say to him, face to face, in person: "Just tell me where you want to go. I'll buy you a ticket, and …"

What ran through my head was how he ruined the second chances that had been offered—ranch jobs, forgiveness, rehab. Living with family, and most recently residing with me, in my studio. But, his addiction always took over.

Hesitation seems to linger before a person says something harsh or mean, and even if I didn't notice it then, it was still there before I spoke. "And I never want to see or talk to you again."

I had never talked to my Dad that way—I had kept my cool for some fifteen years by running toward my escape.

The Cowboy stood there, sober, with his cowboy hat tipped a bit, muttering "Sorry." He was also defeated.

My tears were confined within the boundaries of my eyelids, red and eager to blink. My nerves felt like a thousand-piece, glass puzzle, vulnerable to the slightest gust. *Stay strong. Focus. Don't cry*, I thought.

There was no gesture of good-bye. I left the Cowboy at the bus station where he bid farewell to his captivity. I sat in my car, crying as I watched each bus drive away, slowly with a grey cloud of exhaust trailing behind and hesitating with the shifting of gears.

Two

It *was* love at first sight for both of us; the Cowboy was the first to hold me moments after I was born. The twenty-year-old slender face with cowboy features, mustache and a hat; the Cowboy's scent—a bit of cigarettes, the outside air and fresh hay—locked in a newborn's sensory vault, and there, he'd always be present.

Four years after leaving Dad at the bus station, I was sleepy-eyed, in my usual morning rush, teaching files on the passenger seat and coddling my cup of wake-up on my way to work.

"Anything helps. God Bless," the homeless man's cardboard pled in black magic marker that Monday morning.

I quickly pressed the button to roll down the window—I needed air. My unsteady hand pressed against my chest; a surge of heat lead the heartbeats up through my ears.

I prayed for a green light so that I would not have to sit reading "Down On My Luck" in my peripheral view. The scruffy man gripped his sign.

Look away. Look away, I calmly coached myself, taking a deep breath in and blinking quickly to distract the flood of tears.

I had developed "radar" for noticing homeless people blocks away, standing outside the post office or grocery store or at the stop light where I exited from the 101 South to and from work. I could see them from afar, little figures in the distance, but my inner voice—the one trying to tell me I needed to deal with my "daddy" issues—warned me of their presence.

I tapped the steering wheel, noticing lines etched around sunken eyes, his sagging expression and the energy of desperation that surrounded him.

At least that's what I saw; the person next to me could have seen something entirely different—a lazy man who had no work ethic.

I had received letters from the Cowboy—living in Arizona, then Colorado, then Wyoming—but he drifted sporadically and I hadn't spoken with or seen him since he left on the Greyhound bus.

The light finally turned green, and I gunned the gas.

Three

She usually worked during the day, but tips were better at night, so when Dad finished the day's work around 7 p.m., he'd take R.J. and me to have dinner at The Timber Creek Restaurant.

Mom wore a half apron around her waist with pockets in the front, filled with tips, a pen and a waitress pad. The Cowboy would always take off his cowboy hat and tell my brother to do the same if he were wearing a baseball cap. Mom sat down in the extra chair at the table and took our orders.

"Meatloaf and mashed potatoes is the special tonight," she offered, looking at Dad.

Not to flatter, but really seeking her opinion, he asked, "Good as yours?"

"Ya, I was helpin' in the kitchen this afternoon and made it myself," she said with certainty, but no pride. "And I'm guessing Melissa June wants chicken strips with a side of beans and rice and R.J. wants a cheeseburger and fries?"

Dinner lingered longer than usual that night. Mom was too busy taking orders, filling drinks and bussing to visit with us. As my brother and I finished our fries, the Cowboy ventured to the bar on the other side of the restaurant. Our dinner was supplemented with prolonged dessert: apple pie topped with vanilla ice cream.

Just before we left, Dad would draw his thumb and pointer finger down the sides of his mustache, kiss Mom good-bye and when she wasn't looking he would leave a tip on the table.

I hesitated walking out of the door as we left the restaurant; I wanted to make sure she got the tip—a gust of wind could have blown it off the table when the restaurant door opened, or perhaps she wouldn't see it and I would need to point it out.

Really though, I just wanted to watch Mom come back to the table to see the tip—she would smile, look up toward the door and wave good-bye to us, then stuff the dollar bills into her apron. I loved seeing that interaction between the Cowboy and the waitress.

Soon, though, my developing seven-year-old intuition was uneasy, and I squirmed in the front seat of the truck. R.J. was next to me and we looked straight ahead—our view: the glove compartment and radio dial. The stick shift was eye-level and the gears written on the knob were faded.

Dad took the back way home on the winding, wash-boarded dirt road, causing a rackety ride. Swaying back and forth on the vinyl seat around the curves, our little bodies jittered with the grooved road.

The Cowboy swerved the truck and then over-corrected the steering wheel, but recovered without a glitch. Minutes later, the Cowboy drifted into the ditch again.

"Ohh shiit," the Cowboy said, as he swung his arm in front of us as to hold us in place. We didn't wear seat belts back then.

Perhaps it was during these few seconds of shock, my intuition became super hero-like. I held on tight and looked sideways at the Cowboy, who was multi-tasking the situation, gaining control of the truck without appearing too frightened, all while still managing his tipsiness.

Now, my view from the side window was dirt.

"Well, God damn it," the Cowboy said, frustrated, as if he had been bucked off and the bull won.

Our eyes wide and our mouths pouty, my brother and I, holding hands, stared up at Dad.

"That scare ya a little bit? It's okay, you're okay," Dad said reassuring us—and himself—as we just sat there.

Shifting from first gear then reverse, the Cowboy finally got us out of the ditch after a few moments of spitting dirt. The sound of the cattle guard a few moments later meant we were home.

Four

I drummed my fingers on the steering wheel to tunes from the radio. The driver's side window was cracked just enough to let in fresh, spring air. I was twenty-five years old and venturing to a faraway destination, where I knew no one and had no family—the escape I yearned for. I had eighteen hours between Colorado and California to think about my new life.

The last time I was on I-15 South, I was twelve, admiring palm trees from my backseat view, even though then, it was Christmas time.

It had been a year since my "I-will-never-get-over-this" divorce. I'd sold everything—a couch, microwave, TV, bed, kitchen table, knick knacks, pots and pans. I had announced six months earlier that I would be skipping town to Cali (I made this announcement so that I would feel the pressure to follow through with this leap). My brother R.J. had never said a word; honestly, I don't think he believed I would go. And so I crammed my Camry—which I had leased two years earlier with kids in mind—with summer clothes, photographs, my bulky computer, a blow-up bed, and my fluffy, white Persian cat, Abby. She was the only thing I had left from my three-year marriage—oh that and a nice crystal vase and a beautiful pottery bowl for chips and dip. I suppose I should also give credit to the amazing rum cake recipe I got from the ex mother-in-law.

Earlier that day, as I left for Santa Barbara with Abby, my little brother R.J., however, was the one that almost tripped me up. He walked with me along the sidewalk toward the car and in a desperate moment that I didn't expect, he started to cry; he cried bubbly tears and begged, "Please don't leave me. Please."

R.J. was struggling with work, alcohol a little, a void from his past and I thought he was doing ok—just finding his way as twenty-four-year-olds do. I don't know how I found the courage to leave my little brother behind, but I simply said: "I have to do this. I have to go, R.J."

The truth was, it was a well thought-out plan; it had been a year since my (eventually) spirit-saving, emotional divorce. I had roughly $5,000 collected from my "previous life sale" to start anew that June of 2001. I'd always dreamt of living in California. I had the whole rest of my life to figure out a career. And all I kept thinking was, what's the worst that could happen?

After two days of driving, I reached Highway 101 and the Pacific Ocean. As I drove north along the water, I noticed everything—the waves, the humid, salty air, the lushness, and the bright pink Bougainvillea flowers along the highway—who knew a *highway* could be so vibrant! I had never felt this happy and this free. I was laughing, smiling, talking to myself and crying simultaneously; a passerby may have thought I was crazy.

When I first arrived in Santa Barbara, I picked up a day-old *Newspress* at the Daily Grind coffee shop. I quickly found an old cottage to live in with four other roommates—Mike, a kind, retired, realtor in his 60s, who wheezed and coughed through one spoken sentence; another Mike in his late 30s who was a recent, bitter divorced fella; a twenty-something photography student who watched hours of *South Park* when she should have been in the dark room; and another twenty-something who fit the kooky-California-pothead-yoga-vegetarian-astrologer stereotype.

I found Californians so intriguing and interesting with their chill attitude and "Everything is possible if you just open yourself up to it" vibe. This was bullshit mumbo-jumbo where I came from in small town Colorado, but this new California mentality was serving my fantasies well.

Kathleen, the fan of *South Park*, said to me one day casually, "Oh cool, the Santa Ana winds are blowing through."

"What are those?" I asked, as every little detail was a new experience.

"Dude, they're like warm winds. Go outside and see for yourself," she said matter-of-factly, with a shrug.

Valerie, Miss-Mary-Jane-medicated, chimed in, "Ya, it's totally awesome."

I opened the screen door, stepped down the steps into the yard, and a gust of *warm* wind grazed me and twirled through my hair. It was early evening—it *should* have been a cool wind, but instead I was completely giddy from wind: warm wind! As if it were scripted for a sappy movie, I stretched my arms out and twirled around, gazing at the clouds in the sky, my eyes squinting from the sun and a smile. I was like a child experiencing her first snow and feeling the flakes fall on my nose.

"Oh my Gaud, it's just wind," Kathleen said, interrupting my trance, pushing her little glasses up the bridge of her nose. For only a second I was embarrassed by my child-like frolicking with Mother Nature, and then I remembered again where I lived, a dreamy paradise far away from the cold chaos back in Colorado.

"Do you think we could ever live in California?" I'd hesitantly asked my husband two years earlier, holding my breath, waiting for the answer I already knew he would deliver.

"Why would you want to move to *California*?" he said, saying "California" as if it were an infectious disease.

I don't know why he bothered asking; he had no intentions on actually hearing why I would like to move and quickly answered his own question, "You know we can't move to *California*—my family is here."

By "here" he meant *cold* Colorado.

I certainly knew why I wanted to move. I had memories of my childhood road trip to Disneyland in Anaheim California with my parents, R.J. and best friend Kiley. Disneyland was before the pollution of Dad's alcoholism warped the air of our family life. What I remembered was the awestruck wonder of Disneyland, Dad singing "In the teki, teki, teki room" and being in the back seat of the Ford Bronco II, being stuck in traffic somewhere around L.A. and just gazing out the window.

I'm not quite sure what my parents were doing in their front-seat world, but I sat there, unfazed by the unfamiliar bumper to bumper traffic and I dozed off watching the palm trees sway back and forth. Not only did I think that Disneyland *was* the happiest place on earth—I was convinced that *California* was the happiest place. Maybe even then, at age twelve, I knew that I would find my way to California to get lost and find myself.

Five

Johnny Horton played in the background of a small apartment in Littleton, Colorado while Rhonda made pork chops and fried potatoes for Randy, her Cowboy.

Just a few weeks prior, the Cowboy met Rhonda at The Drumstick restaurant, where a model train traveled around the restaurant on a track built near the ceiling. Customers watched the train choo-choo through a scenic, Colorado mural in the dining room, heading toward the kitchen and through a tunnel, all to make the path again.

Rhonda took quick orders in her short dress and apron that curved around her hips; she was eighteen and her long, wavy dark hair was pulled back in a bun, with wispy strands dangling on the sides. Her perfect penciled-in brows made her green eyes pop.

"Let's just get married and have babies," the Cowboy proposed to Rhonda only after a few home-cooked meals and dessert.

The Cowboy and the Waitress were married at the Justice of the Peace on November 6, 1974; they stood in front of the judge and next to their witnesses, Rhonda's parents.

"So what is your new last name going to be anyway?" Rhonda's dad, a truck driver, leaned toward her and asked.

Rhonda hesitated and gazed at her Cowboy.

"She's marrying a God damn cowboy and she doesn't even know his name!" her dad said as Rhonda's mother rolled her eyes.

Rhonda leaned toward the Cowboy, with a sweet smile, and whispered in his ear, "Honey, what's your last name?"

Nine months later, just outside Blanca, Colorado—population a couple hundred or so in 1975—it was a bumpy ride along the washboard dirt road that hot July day, but speed was essential. The old Ford screeched onto the double lane highway; the wide open space, the outline of the Great Sand Dunes and the Sangre de Cristo Mountain range were in the distance as they fishtailed to the nearest hospital in Alamosa.

A baby brother came along eleven months later.

<hr />

Nestled in the San Luis Valley, at the base of the San Juan Mountains, Del Norte is a one-stoplight town of about 2,000 people, mainly ranchers and farmers. I had just turned six when we moved to the Flying W Ranch. Our new home was a brand-new trailer, which was purchased for my family as part of the job. We had come from the Gingerquill Ranch near Encampment Wyoming; we'd been cozy in a one-bedroom cabin with an out-house in the back of the cabin. A watering tank had sat in front.

At only thirteen-years-old, the Cowboy started working on the Flying W Ranch in Colorado Springs, Colorado. He and his cousin/best friend Jim Broughton made biscuits for the chuck wagon dinners. Dad was the second oldest of seven; he had three sisters—Sandy, Teresa, and Kathleen and one brother, Riley—Kathleen and Riley being twins. Dad's parents divorced just as Dad was headed into his teen years. His mom remarried and along came two step siblings, another brother and sister. Dad was the only cowboy in the bunch.

Colorado Springs, with a population of around 70,000 in the 60s, perhaps seemed too city for a little boy who wanted to be a cowboy. Situated near the base of Pike's Peak, "The Springs" was a good place to raise a family. Dad's family had a nice home with a yard and a Scottish terrier named T.W. who howled when you sang Happy Birthday. Years later when my family visited, I played air hockey in the basement and Grandma taught me a song on the piano; it was in the room with plush, white carpet. Dad's stepdad, whom I knew as my Grandpa Tom, owned a bicycle shop. He seemed grumpy, but air hockey and a piano in a house with upstairs and downstairs and white carpet seemed pretty nice to me.

So I'd heard about the Flying W, and now it was real. A lone, old cotton tree stood in the front yard unaccompanied. I sat Indian-style in the grass and watched Dad test the strength of the high branch; he threw the thick rope over the branch and tied a tractor tire to the end.

"Give 'er a try," and with that I put my little body through the tire and would swing, or just sit for hours. The branch would creeeeek, but it was strong. I loved the tire swing until I couldn't fit into it anymore.

———◆———

I soon made a new friend—Kiley and I met at naptime in kindergarten; Mrs. Janis knew we weren't sleeping, and she let us whisper back and forth from our cracked vinyl nap mats. Since we were six years old, Kiley and I were inseparable. We both had long brown hair and freckles. She was more of a tomboy, wore jeans and loved horses, while I was prissier, loved dresses, Strawberry Shortcake dolls, the color pink. She tried to convince me to wear jeans, but I only gave in to the jean jacket because hers looked so cool on her. Kiley had a cool waterbed, and I had a daybed with a ruffled bed-skirt. We proudly shared the same "boyfriend" in first grade—for Christmas he gave me an envelope with ten pennies and Kiley a used Carmex.

One night when I slept over at her house, Kiley asked, "Why do you have holes in your socks?"

"Because of the knots," I said, stating what I thought was the obvious. As young as I could remember, up until 3rd grade when I dressed myself, Mom bought me knee-high socks.

"Here, put these on Melissa. Now hold still," Mom would say, using big scissors to cut the knots at each end of the seam where the toes were. "Now doesn't that feel better? No knots!" she'd say with a smile and a sigh of relief. It wasn't until much later that I realized that Mom had a sock-knot fetish of sorts. I got new socks a lot and I just had always assumed that Kiley did too.

We may have had our sock differences, but Kiley and I had the same short ice-skating skirts perfect for twirls. Wearing mittens, coats, skirts, skates and only tights to cover our little legs, Kiley and I would stand by the pond anxiously waiting and watching as the Cowboy plowed several feet of snow off the surface. He figured if the pond were frozen enough to hold the tractor, it was safe for two little girls to skate and spin. We often made our own routines, quite certain we would both be the next Dorothy Hamill.

Just to make sure it was safe to skate, after plowing, the Cowboy would walk on the ice, which was quite slippery in cowboy boots. The Cowboy, who had been herding cattle that very morning, was now sliding on the ice with his boots and hat on, pretending to be a skater.

"Hey girls, watch this trick!" Dad said as he glided his boots into a tippy-toe and then twirl, the cattle dog barking and nipping at his heels.

When we were eleven, Kiley and I would ride our bicycles into town from the ranch—about a five-mile ride; it seemed like a real adventure to us every time we took the journey into the small town of Del Norte. These were the cool, "teenager" bikes back then—Kiley's was purple and mine pink; they were fancy bikes for small town ranch girls, but Kiley and I remembered the day the local hardware store got the bikes. They were displayed in a window just off the main street across from Jack's corner market where I could go in anytime and get milk, eggs or other groceries Mom asked me to get. "Just put it on my parent's account" I'd say with a sweet tart sucker in my mouth. (The suckers were only a quarter and I always grabbed one out of the candy jar at the register and then I skipped out of the store, with the screen door snapping shut behind me). We'd gazed at the bikes for weeks; they really *did* seem so "city" and we each begged for them and did our chores religiously, finally earning them for our birthdays.

We would pedal our pastel bikes, with tires made for concrete, up a dusty, rocky road, over a cattle guard, continuing on a smooth dirt road.

"Look no hands!" We became experts at riding and balancing, giggling as we passed the house of a cute junior high school boy we knew.

Coasting into Berwick's, we laid our bikes against the old rusty gas pumps— only one worked. We'd discovered something at

Berwick's that we thought was *our* best kept secret. We headed straight for the cooler and felt the cool air on our sweaty hairlines as we reached for a can each of Nehi Peach Pop.

We paid 50 cents each, guzzled the sweet bubbles. Some days our bellies were so full, we used the pay phone outside of Berwick's to call home and Dad would come into town with the ranch truck, load our bikes and take us home.

———◆———

D uane was a tall man with a pudgy face and plump lips. His greasy, grey hair was combed back, and reading glasses sat on his piggy nose. His overalls accentuated his egg shape and his tummy kept the legs of the pants from covering his socks. The shiny, black shoes with thin laces didn't seem to go with the overalls, but I didn't know what would. Reaching his chubby fingers into his pockets, he held open a hand full black jelly beans. This was not the man I saw in a black and white photo with striking black hair, slicked back Elvis-style, a chiseled face with a pouty smirk framed with dark brows and broad shoulders. The photo was of a handsome man being playful and holding my Dad on his lap as if it were for a photo shoot for a lifestyle magazine. I did know that the man offering me candy was my grandfather.

That fall season at the ranch, when Duane visited my family, R.J. and I were only in elementary school, but we'd overheard enough adult comments to understand him to be Dad's real dad. We had absorbed words like "drinker" and "drunk" into our young minds enough to feel awkward around him. I tried staring at him without being noticed; I was intrigued and just couldn't believe he was Dad's dad.

A sidewalk that led into the porch was covered in thick ice; it had snowed, froze over, and was taking its time melting in the shade of the porch. Wobbling and wearing funny black shoes and overalls, Duane slipped and cracked the ice. He was too drunk to feel a thing, but I just stood there, thinking: What do I do with this man who offers me jelly beans?

He only visited for a couple of days, but it was enough; he got to sleep (pass out rather) in my beautiful purple room—snoring and sweating in his sleep. When he left, I remember Dad saying to Mom, "I will never be like that." Those hopeful words stayed alive in my heart for another twenty years.

My grandfather died just a few years later of alcoholism; he was only 56.

Six

Most days, when I came in from playing, I saw mom's Pepsi can sitting on the kitchen table, with a lit cigarette in an orange-brown, thick-glass ashtray—the smoke floating out of the window screen. She would be cleaning—dusting and vacuuming—and every few minutes she would take a sip of the Pepsi and inhale the cigarette, glancing out the window at Dad on the tractor. She taught me how to wash the dishes and I liked it so much that I washed clean dishes that were stacked in the cabinets. I was almost ten and washing dishes made me feel all grown up.

Sometimes in the summer, I got my own Pepsi and we took our pops out to the yard with black plastic garbage bags and we laid in the sun on those bags. Mom could sunbathe for an hour, but I usually only lasted 15 minutes, distracted by a bee or the sweat on my back sticking to the plastic bag. Those days, R.J. was either playing baseball or fishing for minnows in the pond.

Times were good in the evening when Dad came in from work, took off his boots at the door, and sat in his recliner smoking a cigarette. "Who wants to play 'Hide-the-Cup'?" Dad would shout as R.J. and I came running into the living room from our rooms. It was a game Dad made up—we closed our eyes, Dad hid a coffee mug somewhere in the living room (usually on the top of the curtain rod) and then he exclaimed, "Okay, ready! You can look for the cup!" Whoever found it, got to hide it. We always settled down after about an hour of hiding and finding the cup. It was always good timing too; mom's waitressing shift ended after dinner, and we'd hear the truck pull up if we hadn't already noticed the headlights driving down the dirt road.

"Shhh, Mom's home! Pretend you're asleep!" Dad said with a chuckle and the three of us scurried in the living room, bumping into each other, to sit on the recliner, rocking chair or couch and closed our eyes. "Don't start laughing when she walks in the door," Dad whispered knowing by saying it we would start laughing. R.J. and I just giggled and squirmed.

"Ohh, I guess everyone's sleeping," Mom said as she walked in the door.

———◆———

When the arguments first started, they were mostly in the morning while Mom was cooking breakfast to start our school days and the Cowboy's ranch work.

If I wasn't at Kiley's house, I would hide in my room, the door closed to block the unsettling dispute brewing in the country kitchen over the smell of fatty bacon curling up in the frying pan.

My brother would run into my room, and we'd put a drinking glass up to the wall and listen; I think we were surprised by how much we could really hear—an echo-like conversation strained through the paneled wall to the glass and to our ears. Muffled angry talk about too much beer, passing out in the barn, and stealing hard alcohol from the owners of the ranch house. Mom did most of the talking and the Cowboy kept quiet and agreed to never do it again. (This pattern lasted several years, so much so I learned that "never do it again" meant "I'll do it again and again.")

At first the fights confused our young minds, made us nervous— like we were going to get into trouble, even though we knew we hadn't done anything wrong. Or had we? R.J. and I didn't talk about these fights; we would just listen intently through the glasses and then drop the glasses from the wall, looking at each other as if to say "Did you just hear that?' or "What do you think that means?" We had an unspoken agreement, a shared bond of uncertainty.

Later, in our teen years, R.J. would become a part of the arguments, standing up for my mom. Despite being in my room, I felt myself siding with the Cowboy; he sat quiet and I felt bad that Mom and R.J. were both against him. Still, I did not openly choose sides; I would continue to secure my sanity by isolating in my room, this time, not listening through the wall, just dreaming of graduating from high school and escaping.

When the breakfast fights started, I was about twelve. One day, sitting on the end of my bed, Mom visited my room and started asking for my advice about my dad, our lives, her marriage. She casually just sat on my bed with me or some days she would stand in the bathroom while I was putting on my blue mascara.

"Do you understand what your dad is doing? What do you think I should do?" she asked after a particularly drawn-out fight. Her hair was down and the curls were soft, sitting on her shoulders that rolled inward. She was wearing a light pink sweater unintentionally matching her frosty pink nail polish. Her green eyes were weary and she bit her pink nails.

Initially I was confused, then surprised as I thought, *how cool that an adult is asking for my advice.* And yet, even then I was aware that I was just a kid. I didn't realize that Mom didn't have experience dealing with the situation—Dad's alcoholism. She was the second oldest in a family of ten kids; when she was fifteen years old she quit school and ran away from home and started waitressing. She had only been a teen herself when she started her own family so how could she know what to do? Neither of us could have known.

Still, I remember thinking really hard at that moment for some magic words to offer her.

I don't even remember what "advice" I came up with, but I recall feeling the need to be nurturing, convey a comforting tone. Whatever I said—or maybe how I said it— worked: I could see mom felt reassured and calmer. It made me feel good, superior, all-grown up, helpful, and I started to internalize the pressure to be all of those things to everyone. I could live comfortably in chaos, I figured, if only I could learn to control it.

When Dad disappointed me (and himself) he usually made a peace offering to me—a gift the day following a binge. His pride would not allow him to say "I'm sorry", so the gifts did the job. Was I accepting the drinking by accepting the trinket apologies? Or so I often thought as I admired the gold-rimmed, porcelain cup with a hand-painted cat on my dresser. I would never drink out of it; it was made just to be pretty.

———◆———

I was in 7th grade when my parents told my brother and me that we were leaving the ranch and moving to Bullhead City, Arizona. Dad would get a "regular" job, and Mom would waitress. This seemed to be the start of their race to beat—or hide from— the alcoholism that they convinced themselves was caused by the

Cowboy's dreams of never owning his own ranch, or having his own cattle, or winning the rodeo.

I knew there were unspoken problems with my parent's relationship and the Cowboy's "beer" problem, but even at thirteen-years-old, this move to the desert seemed absurd. The Cowboy had always worked and lived the ranch life and ranching involved more than just a Monday through Friday 8-5 schedule and a monthly salary with benefits. Being a rancher meant working hard all day, dawn to dusk, depending on the time of year. Small town ranchers, who don't own their own ranch, are paid a low monthly salary, but housing and a ranch truck are provided to supplement the pay.

Just days before we left for the desert, everything was packed and our home empty. I walked through the kitchen and stared out the picture window like I always had to see if anyone was driving down the dirt road to visit us.

In the front yard, Mom was piling clothes—mainly jeans—stacking them higher and higher. She seemed in a trance of sorts.

What the heck is she doing? I worried.

Like a film in slow motion, I watched as my mother poured gasoline on the pile of clothes. Then she torched them! A Levi bonfire in my front yard! Symbolizing the ranch life and their wise decision to move away from their problems, obviously caused by denim.

My eyes widened and I hurried out the screen door, screaming, "Mom! Mom!"

She stared at the smoking pile, and then snapped out of her trance and looked at me. Her hair was wild around her face, and her eyes were distant, trapped in the throes of the smoke that surrounded her. I saw the shape of my eyes in hers, my petite frame and narrow shoulders; these were the delicate features, like my porcelain cup, that were pretty and fragile.

"What are you doing? What are you doing!" I insisted.
She didn't have an answer to that, or to anything.

———◆———

M y misplaced family found a stucco house with a yard full of
cacti. All of the neighbors had decorative rocks and succu-
lents in their yards; water was a luxury and it was too expensive to
water lawns. I was always contemplating how this would work out.
I knew Mom would find a waitressing job easily because she was
good at it, and because Bullhead City bordered Laughlin, Nevada;
a river divided the two states and there were plenty of restaurants
in the casinos. As if Bullhead City wasn't already a hell on earth
with its temperatures so hot that people shopped, worked and ran
errands at night, the casino life just across the river drew in an evil,
oppressed community of addicts and poverty. Just as I anticipated,
Mom got a job at Harrah's casino and the Cowboy found a job for
a pool company cleaning the outdoor pools that just about every
stucco house in town had— that is except for ours.

To leave the ranch life with a secure home—lilacs in the summer and ice skating in the winter—in exchange for a dry heat, scor-
pions and small plot with a drab house in a stale neighborhood
seemed crazy-desperate and impulsive, even to a thirteen-year-old.

There was a slight aspect of living in a regular neighborhood—
a mailbox at the end of a driveway— that was intriguing to me, but
that was all. I felt like my mind and body were trapped in a sauna;
I spent my summer days in a boring air-conditioned house and
would go to the grocery store with mom at midnight. I missed
green grass and the purple irises that would grow in the pastures
back home at the ranch. I missed the July Colorado thunder clouds

and cool breeze and the sound of a truck riding over the cattle guard. I missed Kiley.

Before these realizations could even set in, there was a knock at the door. My brother and I were home alone, staying cool inside, while my parents worked. I answered the door and was questioned aggressively by a stranger about my parents' whereabouts; he was particularly interested in their Ford Bronco II.

We were still at the ranch when my parents purchased this "new" vehicle and I remember we were all so excited; that Christmas, Kiley came with my family and we drove, in that Ford Bronco II, all the way to Disneyland. But now, as I faced the beefy man in my doorway, I knew not to say too much, and I played innocent, all the while edging him out of the doorway, wondering why he was so interested in our truck.

A few days later, a tow truck pulled the Bronco away. My parents were at work and my brother and I watched the scene outside the living room window, as the Bronco disappeared past the heat waves in the driveway.

Next thing I knew, I was taking Mom's cigarettes out of the drawer, snuck them and a lighter in my pocket, and ran outside, determined to smoke them. I walked down the street, my anger lit up like a cigarette's cherry. *I'll show them*, I thought stubbornly, "them" of course being the jean-burning mom and pool-cleaning dad—I had only a limited perspective of their adult agony.

I didn't get very far; I didn't know how to work a God damn lighter, was mad at myself for burning my thumb trying, and it was about 107 degrees in hell. So I shoved the cigarette and lighter into my pocket and rushed back to the stale, but air-conditioned house.

That night I wrote Kiley a letter telling her of my terrible week—the tow truck, my failed cigarette rebellion. I waited to mail the letter the following night when Mom went to the grocery store

and there was a mail drop there; it was too damn hot to take it to
the mailbox at the end of my street.

———————◆———————

My parents needed a car to replace the Ford Bronco that had
been repossessed, so they bought an old, white 1970-some-
thing clunker. The engine revved up, and it had red vinyl interior
with tears, a faded black thunderbird outlined on the hood. It fit
Arizona.

But now, in Bullhead City, at a new school—R.J. in 7th grade
and I in 8th—we only had each other, and a shared, bewildering
grief. We were Colorado ranch kids who didn't fit in, and we even
hung out together during lunch break. Just a year before, he was a
pain-in-the-ass that wouldn't leave me and my cheerleader friends,
practicing at my house, alone at my slumber parties. Now during
lunch, we would find shade, sit next to each other and just wait for
the next class and the end of the day.

"What's gonna happen? How long do you think we'll have to
stay here?" R.J. would ask.

I didn't have an answer; I just shrugged my shoulders, "Dunno."

The culmination of these events whipped our spirits, and just
in time my parents realized we needed to leave for survival of our
family. Despite being among chaos, stress and uncertainty, I didn't
see evidence of Dad drinking while we were in the desert— maybe
we did leave the alcoholism behind at the ranch? Or maybe the
Cowboy wasn't cleaning pools after all.

The owner of the Flying W Ranch, Russ Wolfe, was relieved
to hear from the Cowboy and offered him his job back. We were
back at the ranch by June—same house, same job, same town, like

we never even left. I remembered the story of the train that circled the dining room of the Drumstick restaurant; I wondered if we would keep going in circles. It was familiar and comfortable. The lilacs, the Colorado breeze, and my tire swing were all still there, but I wondered if the grass would grow over the charred patch left in the yard.

Seven

The empty bottle of cough syrup on the counter that morning signaled an internal alarm. There was something more than just a cold going around in September. I was only a freshman in high school—I had no clue that one could get a fix from something in the bathroom cabinet.

The day before, Dad had been helping me with cheerleading practice. With his cowboy garb on, Dad clapped and shouted, "Ready! Okay!" I giggled and rolled my eyes; it actually never got old. That was yesterday.

Small town high school life was busy with weekend games, and afterward, cruising the one-mile strip through Del Norte with friends who had their licenses, passing through the only stoplight, and lots of making out with my boyfriend, Jakey, at the drive-in. Jakey was a stellar student and the star athlete. I knew him in junior high, but we didn't start dating until I was a freshman and he was a sophomore. He was tall, dark hair, blue eyes: good-looking. All the girls wanted to date him in our high school of a whopping 170-something. He wore a letter jacket and a class ring.

I had built a corral around the perfection of my teen life and managed to keep the gate closed and Dad's alcoholism safely outside my fence. The whisper was there—the one that said, *I think you should probably be worried about this*, but, like the cheerleader I was, I performed a genuine balancing act. I made the alcohol "mishaps" a part of a typical day, as if finding the Cowboy drunk in the tractor was just the same as doing homework that day—I didn't like either one, but I managed to deal with both.

It was a fall afternoon; school was out and volleyball practice hadn't started yet, so the arrangement that week was for Dad to pick me up at the high school. That plan worked well Monday, Tuesday and Wednesday, but Thursday brought a challenge.

The Cowboy was late; my intuition hissed, "Somethin's up."

I waited nonchalantly as friends and a teacher offered a ride: "Everything okay? Need a ride somewhere?"

I simply smiled, assuring them the Cowboy was on his way. I'm sure they had their doubts as there are no secrets in a small town. It wasn't gossiped about openly, but privately, I'm sure, in the homes of my friends and those who knew my dad. Dinner discussion was often about somebody else in town; my dad being late to pick me up was probably a five-minute conversation over mashed potatoes and fried chicken. As in: "Ya, I saw Melissa Broughton waiting for her ride … probably her Dad drinkin' again. Poor girl, did you hear from his foreman's wife that he was passed out in the barn? Pass me the corn, would ya?"

When Dad finally pulled up to the front of the high school in the ranch truck, his arm hung out the window, thumb and finger grasping a dead cigarette. His sunglasses and hat were cock-eyed. Slivers of hair stuck to his sweaty forehead.

I knew what drunk smelled like—a mix of cotton mouth, stale beer, and body odor from being passed out in the hot, musty truck.

No biggie, I thought, and with that I asked the Cowboy to scoot over so I could practice my driving. He refused. Okay, he was a bit stubborn and there was no need to upset anyone—I would just be on alert, with my seat belt on, while we made the short five mile ride home to the ranch, a drive that he could probably have done it with his eyes closed anyway. He tried to play it cool—always thinking I didn't know when he was drinking and asking me questions about school.

"You and Kiley have cheerlead this weekend?" he said red-nosed, chewing peppermint gum to mask his slur.

He had the window rolled down and his arm resting on the ledge. He re-lit his cigarette and balanced his drags with shifting and steering.

I was impressed, yet slightly annoyed. I still liked talking with him and telling him about my day; I knew he was truly interested—tipsy or not.

"Yep, we have cheerleading," I said, sarcastically.

"Whoa!" he said as if he were halting a horse, weaving and just missing a street sign.

I waited until we got out of town, and had crossed over the bridge that covered the Rio Grande River. "Hey Dad can you pull over so I can practice driving pleeeaaase," I begged, playing the naïve teenager.

"Well, suuure. I reckon so," he said with heavy eyelids; I think the peak of the drunk was kicking in: perfect timing.

Dad pulled the truck over and as we got out of the truck to switch seats, two high school boys, who were *Juniors*, but were friends, stopped and asked, "Everything okay, Melissa? Do you need any help?"

By this time, the Cowboy was already sitting on the passenger side, half passed out.

"Oh ya! Everything's great! I'm just getting to practice driving a stick shift!"

It wasn't an act—I really was excited to drive and I had everything under control with only two more miles home. So I pushed my embarrassment aside.

I didn't need anyone's help.

Eight

I was eighteen when I left the ranch. I graduated high school with awards and honors and couldn't drive away quickly enough on that dirt road to college to continue my plan of creating my own life. Mom, Dad, R.J. and I, had lived on the Flying W Ranch for twelve years; I left for college, but left behind an incomplete family who, even though I had no idea at the time, seemed to depend on me— that fourth strong pillar to hold everything together.

Naively, I thought leaving home and moving forward towards "normalcy" would be my escape from what had become the daunting guessing game of the disease in my teen years. My tendency as an adult to be "too much inside my head"—to overthink everything today—probably stems from the questions and rationalizations I constantly practiced in my youth.

Within a year of my leaping out of my small-town life and toward the city of higher education and hope, my parents and brother left the ranch too. My parents misplaced themselves in Fort Collins, the same town where I went to college at Colorado State University. They found a job taking care of a run-down, 70s apartment complex located behind a grocery store. Mom still waitressed at night, and Dad did okay with the handyman duties for the complex.

The job and housing benefits of the cement apartment complex, with low ceilings and stained carpet, were a far cry from the cowboy job and housing benefits the ranch offered my family. The ranch gave us fields and flowers; the complex painted parking spaces for each tenant. The ranch gave us a home, a yard, the river, fresh air and space to skip and play. The cracked stucco complex offered a patch of grass here and there and shelter. I was only about one mile away, living on the CSU campus in a dorm: my own little cement box complete with stained carpet, a parking space, and the smell of burnt popcorn and old socks.

And there, started a simple pattern—my Mom and her Cowboy bounced around from job to job throughout Colorado. For my parents, a restaurant was always hiring a good waitress and someone always needed a handyman. These were perfect jobs to not get too settled in to; if the drinking started up again, then it was on to the next distraction from the disease. After several years of attempts to gain a life and love once had and felt, my parents left Colorado for good. Eventually they made their way to Wyoming, where they would live for the rest of their lives, but ultimately apart from one another.

———◆———

When I was a sophomore in college, I, on the other hand, decided to settle down—for good. I married my high school sweetheart, Jakey. He told me he loved me when he was sixteen and I was fifteen. Even then, I always knew we would get married, and our teachers would always say so, too. "Ain't love grand" Mr. Jackson would tease us when he saw Jakey standing at my locker leaning in for a kiss. The other high school couples got into trouble for PDA. Not only did Jakey adore me and give me the attention I yearned for, he was finishing high school, had no interest in rodeo or ranching. He had *goals*—he even wanted to go to graduate school. (I knew I would go to college, but I didn't even consider graduate school for myself.) Jakey was trustworthy and responsible. He never got into trouble, never did any drugs and may have had a few beers in high school. Back then it seemed not a conscious effort to marry someone who was the opposite of my dad, but rather secure my escape.

So my college experience was shared with marriage. Kiley and I both married our high school sweethearts within two weeks of one another and we were in each other's weddings. The bigger issue was that my brain couldn't even fathom not going through with it—marriage—it was meant to be. I was under the pressure of my own carefully laid plans. Though now I ponder those pieces of paper with pretty, burgundy cursive inviting people to a "really bad idea," even then I felt reluctance nipping at my heels of my white, satin shoes, and simply I fanned it away with denial and a smile.

It was just a few days before Christmas in 1997 and my new husband and I were visiting Del Norte, at his parent's house to celebrate the holiday. I was Grinch-like, and deeply lacking holiday spirit. My parents had split up again—they'd been on and off for a few years—and both found themselves in Cripple Creek, a mining town turned gambling town. Waitress jobs were plentiful and alcohol was free, along with a cup of peanuts. I was depressed about my family and had another uneasy feeling about my Dad again. And just as my gut alarm rang, low-and behold, the Cowboy called me at my in-laws.

He was at a bar, but luckily carried my phone numbers in his wallet. His speech was slurred and his voice sad; he blubbered that he had just been in a fight.

I tried to gather more info: "Where exactly are you in Cripple Creek? What are you doing? Where are you going?" It was clearly too many questions for a Cowboy down on his luck at Christmas; he mumbled something and hung up the phone.

I was looking for any excuse to escape the in-laws, but more so, Dad's call felt like a cry for help. Concerned for my dad, but also getting to him while driving in the snow, I'd hoped Jakey would offer to take me; he didn't. So I decided to take the three-hour drive to Cripple Creek in the storm to find my dad.

Big snowflakes fell slowly on the windshield as I drove the truck through an old mining, mountain town. The headlights on the falling flakes made for a blinding effect, and my fingers gripped the steering wheel tight, and my squinting eyes followed the snow-packed streets. I found myself alone driving over Poncha Pass, seeing semi-trucks pulled over on the side waiting out the storm. As the sun faded, the half-melted snow started freezing again and icing over the highways. I had just made it far enough over the pass before they closed it, signs warning that chains on tires were needed.

I cried the whole way, sensing that I was being guided by a higher power who towed me over the icy highway pass, led me into the conspicuous town of Cripple Creek. The street lights barely glowed as they were covered with snow. I looked for any sign of the Cowboy. I parked the truck in a spot that appeared as though it were waiting for me; I sat there with the heater running— it was still and the heaviness of the snow seemed to muffle any sounds. What am I doing? How did I get here? How will I find him?

"Just drive," I said out loud.

So I continued down the street, lined with tiny casinos. The lights from the slot machines glared through the snow covered windows. Up ahead, on the right side, I could barely see through the falling snow, a man with a cowboy hat and a limp. I knew it was Dad.

I pulled over, hopped out of the truck, and covering my head with my coat, cautiously paced on the ice, skipping to a fast jog so that I could catch up to him.

"Dad? Dad?" I asked as I cut him off—it *was* the Cowboy with a bloody lip and swollen-shut, black eye.

He was quite drunk, which was a good thing I suppose given his painful predicament. He was also in a drunken disbelief his daughter was standing there in front of him in Cripple Creek when just hours before I was safe and uneasy in a warm and uncomfortable house in Del Norte, 200 miles away. Actually I was in my own disbelief, but yet there we stood.

As the years went by and the Cowboy continued choosing the path toward another rock bottom, each "major incident" added to my shield of protection and lessened the shock value. The DUIs, the broken hearts, the sincere apologies and endless forgiving—all were closing that window of hope. The idea of rock bottom is a source of hope, maybe a source of false hope, and I was starting to wonder what it would take for the Cowboy to have an epiphany, a rock bottom moment?

The next thing I knew we were sitting at a bar in one of the casinos warming up. It had been two years since I had seen the Cowboy, and now I understood where the Cowboy was getting his calories—whiskey and mixed nuts.

Forgetting everything I learned about living with an alcoholic for a moment, I started asking all of the "why" questions again, mainly how and why he got in a fight. It was no use, of course, and in the next second I realized I just needed to "be" with the Cowboy.

We sat at the bar; he was slumped over and I was rubbing his back. And even though I discouraged it, the bartender poured whiskey to the top of a tall coffee mug and added a splash of coffee. Small talk with the bartender revealed that the Cowboy was a regular as was this drink of choice.

I sat on the stool a little stumped and sighed, focusing on the foggy window, and somehow, had a brief moment of serenity.

After a slight "nap" on the bar, Dad eased into the beginning of soberness; this was my opportunity to offer my help, even if I knew deep down he wouldn't take it.

"Come back with me," I said.

Nine

I was twenty-eight and living in a small studio in Santa Barbara. It was situated behind a house; a small pathway, over-grown with jasmine, led to my front door. It was about 300 square feet with a petite bathroom and kitchen nook, French doors that looked out to the small yard and a loft where I slept. California had taught me how to simplify, go without and live minimally and I thrived in that philosophy; it made change and adapting easier. I learned I could do and live without a lot and I rarely missed what I donated or sold. No attachments and nearly everything was replaceable. I was and had been overwhelmed by California since day one of arriving to town –it was overstimulation of the senses and perhaps I hadn't realized it because most of it was extremely new, beautiful and positive. But California had taught me to filter; I learned quickly to filter things out that were of little importance and no use to me. If I couldn't change a stressor or worry, I would filter it out. It may have been avoidance or denial, but it's how I survived.

I had just finished graduate school in L.A. where I lived in a studio on top of a garage. Now I had a master's in education administration, a cottage studio, a job at a private photography college in Santa Barbara and a nice-guy boyfriend with a bit of a California vibe –independently wealthy, his parent's retired surgeons, he drove a BMW like the rest of Santa Barbara. Nice-guy was also good-looking; he was witty and silly and after meeting him, people would say, "Wow, what a nice guy." My life was far removed from my small-town days.

———◆———

I talked with Dad on the phone—sometimes he was sober. At first he stayed with his sisters in Arizona, but eventually made his way to Wyoming where he went from job to job–building fences or branding cattle at various ranches or handyman work at restaurants and hotels. He either got injured or fired, both from drinking on the job. He spent the little money he had on food, cigarettes and liquor. He admitted to living under a bridge in Laramie for a short time. Since we were co-dependent, as the phrase goes, I couldn't help but try to intervene, and he couldn't help but give me the opportunity. His need made me feel useful, strong, like the loving daughter I knew I was. Living in Santa Barbara, I was surrounded by horse/ranch country—to the south of Santa Barbara was Ojai—a small town with horse ranches, but also an artist and hippy vibe; further south was Thousand Oaks, definitely a horseman's territory with big horse ranches abound with the city growing inward like unstoppable weeds. To the north of Santa Barbara—the Santa Ynez Valley and Los Alamos, just to name a few cow towns— were in wine country. I researched local papers, Craigslist and I even subscribed to the *Caretaker Gazette* (a newsletter listing ranch, travel and temporary jobs all around the world.)

My desire to help led me to a "perfect" job for my Cowboy Dad. A small horse ranch in Thousand Oaks was looking to hire a horseman; as a typical ranch job would have it, pay and furnished housing were included. The small ranch was owned by an older fella and his wife. I sent an email and resume to this gentleman about my dad (explaining that my dad had no access to email).

Soon the Cowboy was on a bus from Colorado, to Thousand Oaks, California, for a fresh start. The owner had arranged to pick up the Cowboy at the bus stop and I would drive to meet them. I hadn't seen my Cowboy Dad for four years, and I had realized that my theory of getting over the loss of my family would get better as I got older, was dead wrong, in fact, exactly the opposite. The older I got, the more I missed my dad.

We'd arranged to have dinner together at the horseman couple's house the night my Dad arrived. As Highway 101 took me south into Thousand Oaks and I exited, the highway and city surroundings became more scenic and rural. I could see where this used to be open country with horses and how suburbia had closed in and local horseman benefited financially from development. Finally, arriving on the property, the road was a dirt road, which strangely felt familiar and eased my tension a little.

I rang the doorbell; the horseman's wife answered the door and sweetly introduced herself, "Well, hello dear, you must be Melissa. I'm Mary."

Standing behind her was Bob, the husband, and he seemed like a jolly fella; both were a bit plump, wore glasses and seemed to be content, happy folks. On the outside I stayed graceful and calm, but inside I was just waiting for that moment I would see my Dad appear— and within seconds, there was my Cowboy, dressed in the only "outfit" I had ever seen him in: jeans, boots, and a ring around his brown hair from his hat. We both contained our excitement and showed just the right amount of attention—the horseman couple didn't know we hadn't seen each other in years, nor did they have an inkling of the Cowboy's drinking problems.

"Well, hey there young lady," Dad said with a smile and a cup of coffee in his hand. I was happy to see him with a cup of coffee and a smile; the last time I saw him he had whiskey hidden in a coffee mug and a bloody lip in a Cripple Creek bar.

We hugged as a father and daughter would hug as if they just saw each other yesterday, but I wanted to hug him long enough to make up for lost time. As Dad talked about his work and I chimed in with my own memories on the ranch, I wondered: did they notice how Dad and I had the same full lower lip, nose and forehead? Did the old ranch folks see that my mannerisms were the same as Dad's when we told a story—our eyes squinting when we laughed?

We had an early dinner; the purpose was really for the horseman couple to get to know the Cowboy, but it was also the "thing to do"—being ranch folk, it was only good manners to have dinner with the cowboy they just hired to take care of their horses. "Supper" was hot stew and biscuits served with friendly small talk.

What the horseman couple didn't realize is that Dad and I hadn't sat down for "supper" together in a long time, and we were both hanging on each other's every word. It was sort of this funny/awkward secret that my dad and I held at the table. We were perfect together, reading each other's minds, knowing we had to play the part of "normal" father/daughter. Sitting at that table, with a smile on my face, complimenting the Mrs. on her delicious home-cooked meal, I could see an evident sadness in my Cowboy Dad and that little voice in my head dreamed of how I could save him, make him feel happy.

After dinner, we left the couple and Dad showed me his new "housing"—it was a small, furnished cottage with all of the fixings for a humble, but comfortable, new life. A quick trip to the grocery store was in order; the Cowboy hadn't worked in months and had no money, so I bought him some groceries—mainly cowboy necessities: cigarettes and coffee, meat and potatoes.

The Cowboy expressed how "easy" the job would be just taking care of four horses; "This ain't nothin' compared to the Ranch." Dad had managed 400 head of cattle, irrigation for a 500-acre ranch, and went through calving and haying season for thirteen years. Through the years, the Cowboy had also created metal art from barbed wire, horseshoes and other metal pieces he found lying around the ranch. These works of art—I've seen similar pieces sold in art shows for hundreds of dollars—disappeared through the years, probably sold or traded. I wondered if he could use this extra time to make these pieces again—a rusty, barbed wire wreath with an old boot in the middle was a favorite of mine; Dad's former boss Russ Wolfe from the Flying W bought that piece. The piece I really admired, though, was an old shovel head upside down, as if it were a hill. At the top of the shovel-head hill was a tree with a wide trunk and branches sculpted with copper wire and sitting against the tree, in the shade, was a wire cowboy with tipped cowboy hat on. Dad found a little piece of red fabric that he tied around the resting cowboy's neck for a scarf.

Even as we chatted in his cottage, there was never a moment where we really sat down and talked about each other's lives and catching up—that's just not how my Cowboy Dad was, even though I was curious about his life. I noticed his depression that surrounded him like a veil of pollution. I truly felt it and it worried me.

With a smile, I offered all of the good things. "Just think, I'm only an hour away and we can have dinners together and spend time together."

I was hesitant—the daughter's intuition, which had been shaped to be so sharp that I could detect the littlest "offness"—the

Cowboy's movements, tone of his voice, his eyes, his words. Still, with a well of hope in my heart, I left for Santa Barbara to resume my normal life.

Ten

D ad lasted two days at the horse outfit. I got a call from the old horseman, and he told me: "Your dad had been drinking a lot I think; the last I saw him he was walking down the dirt road and wouldn't accept any help or a ride; I gave him some money and let him go on his way."

In a controlled panic, I asked, "Oh my, I'm so sorry. Did he say where he was going?"

The horseman replied, "He asked which direction Santa Barbara was," then adding, "You didn't mention a drinking problem. I think your dad is an alcoholic—did you know this?"

"Yes, but I thought he was better, sir. I'm really very sorry for the trouble," I said, with sorrow and shame. And then I said good-bye.

From an outsider's perspective, a non-adult child of an alcoholic perspective, there were obvious problems with my so very logical plan—the Cowboy was in the midst of the most sad time of his life: he had lost his mom, his wife, his job, belongings and as a result of all of that, his identity, sense of self, sense of humor, hopes, dreams, spirit and character. He wasn't gone, but he was lost—a lost cowboy.

And despite the "cowboyness" of the job, Dad was a cowboy from Wyoming and Colorado and California didn't exactly fit his MO.

It was a long day at work, getting the news of the missing Cowboy somewhere between Thousand Oaks and Santa Barbara; I visualized an out-of-place cowboy with his hat and boots hitchhiking or riding on a bus on the 101 Northbound. I got home from work and unlocked the door to my studio, still pondering what the hell I was going to do.

The silhouette of a cowboy hat just a few feet away startled me. It was Dad, sitting on my futon couch, in the dark. I was instantly relieved, but stumbled over my words while scanning the studio trying to figure out how he got in. I could have just asked him, but then I saw the small window by the kitchen sink that had been slid open about two feet. I looked at the small open space of the window, then turned my head to look at the Cowboy to see if he had shrunk since I saw him just two days before. Then I looked at the window again, thinking "Nooo way" and then spilled coffee on the counter and floor revealed where he'd knocked over a cup.

"Dad, geez … how did you get here? How did you know where I lived?"

The Cowboy chuckled, raised an eyebrow, shook his head and glanced at the window he had just crawled through. Had he had more money he wouldn't have been sober, but he was.

———◆———

Dad lived with me for a month. The plan B was a good plan— we'd look for another ranching job in the area and start from scratch (again); for some reason I hadn't accepted the lesson in all my years with the Cowboy that logical plans were like branding a cow without a shoot to hold it in place.

I took the Cowboy to get a haircut and a shave to distract from his disease, which he wore like a mask. Every day I came home from work and there he would be—sitting on the slight porch with the French doors wide open. I enjoyed our time together and our conversations, but I knew he was so sick with alcoholism—it showed in his red face and swollen nose. I slept in the loft and he slept on the futon couch and it was a reasonable set-up to figure things out.

I dated Nice Guy for about four years; I realized in the later part of our relationship that nice guys can still be emotionally un-available… in their own polite way. Still, I was comfortable around Nice Guy; besides the ex-husband, Nice Guy was the only boy-friend who had met Kiley when she visited me in California before she got sick. Nice Guy's kind character allowed me to be vulnera-ble and share about my dad –both were charismatic and both had a joyful laugh so powerful, I knew the two of them meeting would be a positive experience. Nice Guy eventually turned into "I thought he was 'the One'" guy.

Nice Guy wanted to prepare a salmon dinner for Dad and me and so we made dinner arrangements that day after work.

"Pops, he's making salmon for us!" I said when referencing Dad meeting Nice Guy.

"Sounds fancy" Dad said with a smile, but truly thought eating salmon was indeed "fancy". I giggled.

Nice guy's apartment was just up the street from my studio.

"After work we'll just walk to his apartment and have dinner."

I was excited all day at work. I thought Nice Guy could be "The One" and so I wanted the Cowboy to meet him. I arrived home from work and the Cowboy was ready for dinner; he seemed in a jolly mood. The Cowboy and I—he in his jeans and cowboy hat and boots and me in my flip flops and sundress walked a few blocks past an old grocery store and corner liquor store. I was a little nervous for my dad and my boyfriend to meet, but mostly excited.

"Well, howdy!" Dad said with direct eye contact, a smile and a firm handshake before I could get out the introduction.

"Nice to meet you finally Randy; I've heard a lot about you" offering the same direct eye contact, genuine smile and hearty handshake.

"Well, don't believe ever-thing ya hear," Dad laughed. Nice Guy laughed.

Now I just felt like my delayed introduction would just be interrupting their instant connection.

"Dad, this is Ricky. Ricky, this is my old pops." Now I was in on their banter.

I was giddy and relaxed around my dad's satisfaction of the salmon dinner and Ricky's questions showing interest in my dad's work as a rancher.

"So you rodeo? What is that even like?" Ricky, a Filipino city-boy from the East Coast, asked sincerely intrigued.

It was going so well. And then it wasn't and just as intoxication started kicking in, I remembered … forgot rather, the corner liquor store by my sober studio. Dad had been alone all day while I was at work. Each minute that went by, it became obvious that he had found company in beer an hour or so before dinner and the buzz was kicking in.

Bantering salmon dinner was over and Dad and I stumbled home, tripping over the cracks in the sidewalk and passing the corner liquor store, where I often stopped to buy a piece of red vine licorice.

I came home from work the next day and the Cowboy had puked all over my living room, which being a studio, was also my kitchen and dining room. The stench was the salmon dinner from the night before at Nice Guy's place; it was all over my futon couch, which was also a bed. Even weeks later, I found chunks of dried vomit hiding in the crevices of my couch-bed and throughout my living room-kitchen-dining room. It was like a clue to a riddle I had already figured out.

Never without another solution, I bargained with the Cowboy, again forgetting that negotiating with a cowboy is like bull-riding— when all is said and done, no matter how long I seem to be able to hold on, eventually I get bucked off.

"Dad, I have been researching rehab places."

He sat in the lawn chair on my mini patio, smoking a cigarette, with no eye contact, staring at the jasmine vines that perfumed my studio when the French doors were open, but now the aroma of jasmine blended with salmon vomit.

"I called and spoke with the director of the Mission Treatment Center. I explained everything to him and he said they have room for you." I paused, hoping for a positive response.

Nothing.

"Dad, it's *free*. They offer housing, counseling, food. And it's close to me." I was excited by something that seemed too good to be true. Hell, I was paying $1000 a month for a box with French doors; I wondered if they had a treatment program for co-dependence.

I felt my heart pounding, but then I remembered the salmon, "Dad, I'm sorry, but I'm not going to allow you to stay here after what happened. This is what I am offering."

Dad simply nodded.

That next day at work I called The Mission Treatment Center in Santa Barbara and made arrangements for the Cowboy to check in.

"And we'll still get to see each other all of the time and the beach is just a few blocks away!"

He did not care about the ocean breeze and stayed one night in my one-millionth perfect solution.

"Melissa? This is Mike here at the Rescue Mission; I'm sorry to tell you this, sweetie, but your dad left. Just said he couldn't handle staying here."

My ears rang with heat. My breathing shortened.

"All he said was that he was going to catch a bus outta town; I imagine he made his way to the Greyhound Station."

My steady sympathy and compassion vanished as I drove to the Cowboy's getaway. I had hit my limit with my intentions, aid, optimism and resources.

I had hit rock bottom.

Eleven

The Flying W was a ghost ranch and from a distance, everything looked the same, as if I could wave and honk to Dad on the tractor in the field, and arrive at the front door, Mom greeting me with a glass of iced sun tea, half an inch of sugar at the bottom of the glistening glass. I was thirty-years-old, and it had been a decade since my family left; I needed to reconnect with the ranch, which was my home and my childhood.

I could see that the fields and pastures needed attention from irrigation and a tractor. The summer breeze would sway the slender grass and wild flowers and give them a little life, but then a dehydrated tumbleweed would sweep across—a sign of what was lost. The sawbuck fences still stood sturdy, but some of the barbed wire fences lost their balance, collapsing in the foxtail grass: a nuisance of a weed for the Cowboy back in the day, as it mixed with the alfalfa bails. He cursed it often, "God damn foxtail!"

The Flying W had fallen victim to a handful of wanna-be cowboys, bad ranch managers that I watched from afar, hearing from Kiley, who lived in Del Norte with her husband and two kids, that the ranch slowly started to crumble and become a ghost ranch. When I found out the ranch was sold to a Texan billionaire, I wanted to fly to Colorado and tie myself to a tree—the tree where my tire swing once was, but that wasn't too realistic, although it may have proven just how California had rubbed off on me.

I drove slowly over the cattle guard; it still made a wonderful noise as I passed through—the sound sparked memories with Kiley, the Cowboy and my home. As I got closer to the houses and barn, I slowed down even more; I rolled down the window and could smell the old hay, hear the crackling of the pebbles under the tires as I rolled to a stop. I got out of the car as if I were in a trance. I walked slowly, noticing every little detail that I didn't notice as a kid, but my heart remembered—an old tire, the water pump with a red handle, and an old wagon wheel placed against the fence. I walked to the place where the pond used to be where Kiley and I would ice skate in the winter and R.J. and I would catch minnows in coffee cans in the summer. It was no longer a sparkling pond, but rather a dried up indention in the earth. I wandered to the old bunk house—the trailer that was our first home when the Cowboy moved us to the Flying W; I noticed the cottonwood tree where my tire swing swayed. I could smell the sweet aroma of my favorite lilac bushes even though they were no longer there. I gazed past the yard and into the pastures and imagined the cattle grazing: I remembered the way the cows would move their mouths, chomping and churning round and round with bits of grass poking out, just another lazy day for them.

Roaming around the ranch took me back to that day in 1986, me and Kiley on our 10-speed bicycles—this was before "mountain bikes" or "road bikes". My 10-speed was black with pink handlebars and Kiley's black with purple handlebars; we didn't notice that our bikes were not "made" for ranch dirt road excursions. I squeezed the handlebar brake, exuding a poof of dust from the warm, fine dirt under my skinny tires made for concrete.

"Kiley! Look!" I whispered excitedly, wide-eyed and stretching my arm fully, pointing at an unsuspecting reptile minding his own business.

Kiley didn't bother with the handlebar brakes and just jammed her feet down from the pedals to the dirt. She gasped, biting her bottom lip and then cupping her hand over her mouth. We were not scared—we were elated. An actual snake!

"Do you think it can see us?" she whispered.

I shrugged my shoulders, not wanting to startle it. We both stood with our legs on either side of our bikes as we gazed at the reptile sunbathing and stretched across our dirt road, prohibiting us to go any further without the danger of getting struck.

"Hey," I whispered again and then I pointed at the snakebite kit in my back pocket with a smile. We took that damn kit everywhere; it was a rubber tube shaped like a giant yellow pill. Inside was a folded and rolled up instruction booklet with a poorly drawn picture of a bare foot. The rubber tube pulled apart, to be used as the suction device to pull out the poisonous venom. (Dad had made sure we were always prepared for the dangers of the Wild West). The kit made us fearless, as if we kept guns in holsters.

The poisonous, *deadly* snake was far enough away—five yards or so—and hadn't moved. Perhaps the snake was indulging us.

"It hasn't rattled yet," I said, expecting a rattle serenade.

"Did you hear that?" Kiley asked, hoping it was rattling.

The Cowboy had enticing snake stories and talked a lot about the rattler itself.

"Look what I found!" he'd once said, climbing down from the horse holding a headless rattle snake. He explained he cut the venomous head off (with his pocket knife or shovel) and buried it.

"'Nuther rattler to add to my collection" The Cowboy had an antique glass bottle he found in the old barn and filled it with rattles from all of his close encounters—while irrigating, fencing, plowing, working in the barn and riding. The cloudy-glass bottle was full of rattles, some bigger than others, displaying the age range of the snakes.

Now we were in the midst of our own encounter.

"How are we going to get around him?"

At that moment the snake seemed to fidget in surprise, pause, and then he slithered into the grass.

That was our snake spot for years to come. And every time we passed by, we hesitated and proceeded cautiously with a giggle.

———◆———

When I came to our old house, I smooshed my face against the windows to see inside the living room; spider webs spread thick like vines in each corner of the window frames. The doors were unlocked, and I did not hesitate going in. *My* house seemed so much smaller than it had when I was a kid and even a teenager— stained carpet, familiar fireplace, wood paneling, and the kitchen's picture window so we could always see who was driving down the dirt road to visit us. I walked down the long hall, where the Cowboy helped me with my cartwheels for hours at a time. I stood in that hallway, closing my eyes to wring out the tears, and tilted my head back as if to the heavens, with a sigh that I'd hoped God would hear.

There were places in the house—a closet, a cabinet, a hidden corner—where I remembered finding empty beer or whiskey bottles. Back then, the bottles had already been hidden by the Cowboy; I found them and hid them again, not understanding my actions, only knowing that the one time I found a hidden empty bottle, showed Mom and ignited a meaningless screaming match.

Some part of me just wanted to move back in right then and there and allow what was left of my broken spirit to live with the other ghosts. I opened the screeching front door that still slammed shut and made my way to the corrals at the barn. This is where the Cowboy hoisted me up on a horse for the first time. "Whoaa, steady now fella," he'd said quietly as he stroked the horse's long nose. My little legs clutched the big belly of the animal and my hands squeezed the horn of the saddle as if my life depended on it. I felt courage from his hand leading the horse and from the pink feather he put in my straw cowboy hat.

I found myself back in the car, taking another dirt road leading through the ranch, past the old, rickety barns along the Rio Grande and passing fields of purple irises. I wasn't supposed to be there, but I felt a sense of entitlement and knew that nobody cared if a sad country girl visited from California and drove down the dirt road once or twice a year to heal her heart.

I visited the ghost ranch a handful of times after all of my schemes for saving my Dad started to unravel. It was therapy to me—visiting the ranch in the summertime, driving out there, by myself or sometimes with Kiley—taking the same walk as I always did, to the pond and barn and back.

With Kiley next to me, we were both silent and I turned off the radio and took in every little detail that I could—the wideness of the dirt road, the hawks flying above, and the sound of the cattle guard as I drove over it. We saw antelope and a rabbit, but Kiley would just extend her arm and point, we still didn't say anything. The wind was swaying the sunflowers in the field, and I felt the warmth of the sun and the familiar. I rolled down the windows and let the breeze enter—that sweet alfalfa aroma always gave me goose bumps.

Kiley leaned out the window to feel the sun on her face. "It hasn't changed, has it?"

We both knew the heart of the ranch would never change; it was still and would always be home.

Twelve

I was in the greeting card aisle of the local drugstore when I realized I'd missed my calling: I should be writing cards for the section called, "Daddy Issues." I mean, I couldn't be alone in feeling that these Father's Day cards were a load of bull. In fact, I personally knew many women who would be right alongside me to contribute their truthfully poetic messages—cheerful and heartfelt with a dose of honest "I feel" statements: real, raw and uncensored. They'd also simultaneously convey all the disappointments and lessons, while acknowledging the good memories and the unconditional love a daughter has for her father. Unconditional, like what I had for my Cowboy—even when I did get mad at him, I couldn't stay that way. That is, unless it was the week before Father's Day and I was searching for a card.

There I was, age twenty-eight, standing among the rows of cheerful, bubble-lettered greetings, pop-up golf-balls and cartoon Dads, contemplating which I should pick. I had already graduated high school, graduated college, been married and divorced to the high school sweetheart that took the Cowboy's place from the time I was fifteen to twenty-four. I will admit, for being just a teenager, the ex did a pretty good job. His fathering ceased when I was about twenty-four, and when he met another woman who showed interest, which I had stopped doing, and perhaps she didn't have "daddy issues" like I had—still trying to be the best, carry the weight of his addiction on my shoulders. So perhaps a Father's Day card, the cover a cattle guard with green pastures in the distance, in my early 20s would have read: *I feel like I am living in chaos, so I left the house as soon as I graduated high school to escape; I went to college to continue the quest for greener pastures still subconsciously thinking that would turn things around. I married too young –A husband I thought was what I needed. I feel worried, stressed and overwhelmed by your drinking. Although I don't realize it now, the thought of this overwhelms my heart, so I'm going to distance myself and try being a good little wife.*

I don't need you. I need to breathe. I need to leave.

In Junior High, that's probably when the cards would've began to stray from the "daddy's little cowgirl" motif as I started to notice warning flags here and there. But still, the Cowboy helped me and Kiley practice our cheers (by mimicking us). Don't all cowboy dads cartwheel alongside their daughters?

Eighth grade was the year from hell—in fact the cover of my card would show flames to represent the Arizona heat or the burning denim my mom torched just before our move to Hades. *No irises or cool breeze. No tumbling weeds rolling in the fields and no saw buck fences. The car has been repossessed and I'm surrounded by concrete, heat waves and cacti. Rebellion gives me permission to smoke a cigarette.* That's card-worthy poetry.

My high school years, the messages, overall, would have revealed my young adult perspective with a slight teenager attitude. *Found you drunk in the barn again. Don't worry I won't tell. I love you like crazy, but I'm so confused. This seems to be really fucking up our family. I'm going to fix this—I feel like I need to be a perfect daughter.* OR maybe: *Since you are not really being a dad to me in my important teen years, I will find a boyfriend to take your place.* I ponder what the cover of this Father's Day card would look like and I can't decide.

Trapped in that aisle among the other customers—sons, daughters, wives, grandchildren—I thought: Hallmark is co-dependent; where are the "real" cards? Like, for example, the one I needed at twenty-five, when I ran off to California. A Father's Day card to my dad when I was 25 (he was 45) would have simply said with a sigh of relief: *I'm divorced. I have no furniture. I have no job. Do you remember the palm trees at Disneyland–swaying back and forth with not a care in the world? I'm getting outta dodge; I'm going to California. I'm not sure where you are or where you're going.*

The cover of the card would be an island surrounded by water, sun shining and I would be shaded by a palm tree.

It wasn't all sunshine. Santa Barbaran's call them "June Gloom" days –but I had more than just a few foggy days in June. These years made me a stronger woman who learned to be even more adaptive and resilient, more likely to take risks and choose adventures, and served me well in the *big* picture. Since I "didn't care" about my family and from age 25ish to 29ish, I fell in love with out-of-my-price-range Santa Barbara and my surroundings, lived with five friendly, obnoxious photography students, wrote a book for first generation college students, finished graduate school, filed bankruptcy, made lifetime friends, and post 9-11 economy made finding a job nearly impossible.

I started "dating" emotionally unavailable men, who, in one cowboy way or another, were unavailable. I was at ease in these relationships and yet a higher-self continued to pierce my heart revealing a sting that something wasn't right with this cowboy or that cowboy. I settled in to a cozy little studio, attained a "now I have a master's degree" job and had a mini, dreamy-at-first window of time with the Cowboy—all the while acknowledging my progress and suppressing my sadness of the "loss" of my family. A Father's Day card to my dad when I was in my late 20s would have said: *The heartache that I feel because you are far away inspires me to achieve many great things. I'm not quite sure what else to say except, "I'm faithful in the process" as Californian's like to put it.*

The cover –a broken heart. That's definitely Hallmark material.

There were a few years that I didn't get around to mailing a card because I didn't know where the Cowboy was roaming. I still tortured myself by visiting the card aisle in June. Had I gotten a card though, it would have said: *I wonder where you are. Do you wonder where I am? I like to imagine you are riding a horse in a big pasture in Wyoming.*

Much later, in my early 30s, I would have penned a rebelliously sweet type of card; it would actually mirror a card I would have written for my dad when I was little—when all I could see was his beauty and grace: my hero who wore a cowboy hat. The only difference would be that when I was little, I didn't realize how cool it was to have a cowboy Dad to scrape ice off the pond with a tractor so I could ice skate or get me a pink feather for my cowboy hat. I assumed that all fathers did stuff like that. The cover of the card would be a cartoon girl, smiling as she lay on the grass, looking up at the clouds, a pink feather floating through the breeze. The inside of the card –*Acceptance.*

But I was still a few years away from those types of cards. So that day, though I usually kept my emotions controlled and at bay, there was just something about those cards that made me want to scream; I literally kicked the card stand (looking around first to make sure no one was around), all while gritting my teeth and, under my breath, cussing, "Are you fucking kidding me? This is a bunch of bullshit. Fuck, I hate this!" as I read each word—*always, forever, hero, role model, best, most*. I wanted to rip the cards into pastel confetti, hurling them into the pharmacy, tossing them through the feminine care aisle! I was so fucking incensed that there wasn't a single card that stated the simple truth (okay, complicated truth). Some started out with a good beginning "Through the years…" and then all went to hell after that. In the section read, "To father from daughter" I chose a card with a general picture of a river, read it—nope, no fucking way—and shoved it back into the slot. I tried another—this one with a picture of deer; he would like that. Then I started reading and let out a "Grrrr" and forced it back into the slot. Then I would look around at kids and adults looking for a card and it made me sad. Finally I picked up a card, that still, was not suitable for the Cowboy, but with words that made me cry— miss, love, care, memories.

With puffy eyes, I eventually left the drugstore with a blank card so that I could just write a message—a nice but simple one, no clichés. Fuck Hallmark; I'll write my own. I wrote: *I remember when* and then followed it with ten bulleted beautiful memories and then summarized the end with *all of the special things you did for me*. I wanted to focus on the good and I thought it would make him feel good.

In retrospect, I think it did.

Thirteen

"**B**uckhorn Bar," the voice on the other end said with a Wyoming twang. I heard the clanking of bottles and glasses in the background.

"Um, yes. Hi," I said, took a deep breath. "I know this is going to sound like a strange question, but do you know someone there named Randy Broughton? I'm Melissa ... his daughter."

Slight awkward pause. "Er ... emm," from the bartender.

"He'd be a local customer?" I asked, hopeful.

"Anyone know-a Randy Broughton?" he yelled away from the receiver. "Oh, you mean Rowdy?" he asked, returning to the phone.

My heart jumped like a colt. "Yes, yes, ya, Rowdy, that's him. He there?"

"Rowdy's not here now, but he does come in jus-bout ever day."

I couldn't believe it! Bingo! Relief! For a moment, I even forgot that, well, I just found my Dad in a Wyoming *bar*.

Giddy, I thought an explanation was necessary to get this bartender to help me. "Well, I'm his daughter and I've been looking for him, and, like, I'd like to talk with him. Would ya mind if I called back?"

"Ya, I reckon you can call back, but let me give ya some advice— call before 3:00, he won't be drunk yet."

That one-sentence advice from a friendly bartender revealed where the Cowboy would be both physically and emotionally. Which helped me prepare the tone, pitches and careful words I'd approach the Cowboy with after not seeing—or speaking to him—for four years.

I didn't rehearse too much what I would say; I was too occupied anticipating the sound of the Cowboy's voice. I sat there with the phone to my ear, which radiated anxious heat; I could feel a little sweat on my cheek touching the phone. My hands shook just a little as I dialed the next day before 3:00, and listened.

"Yep, he's here," the bartender said as if he was expecting my call.

"Hey Rowdy?" the bartender yelled as if the Cowboy were at the end of the bar; I visualized the bartender nod his head to get his attention.

He raised his voice so the Cowboy could hear over the other wranglers—"Says she's your daughter? Melissa?"

It was as if someone hit the mute button; the silence and pause allowed my ears to become my eyes; the pause showed the bartender raising a shoulder up to his ear as if to say, "Hey, I dunno … I just work here."

And a picture of the Cowboy's face, as if to say, "Who me?" with a raised eyebrow. Dad and I hadn't talked since that day at the bus station in Santa Barbara.

I could almost hear the energy shift as Dad moving toward the phone behind the bar, with each step thinking, *you got the wrong cowboy.*

"Uh … hello?"

It was a sober hello; I knew this hello well, but didn't have time to be relieved. I could feel the tears at the corners of my eyes.

"Hi Dad, it's Melissa."

"Well, I'll be damn," the Cowboy said, happy tone of disbelief and a half chuckle mid-sentence; I imagined his smiling eyes.

My shoulders relaxed a bit as I said, "How are ya Dad? I miss ya and it's good to hear your voice."

It was the perfect combination of letting the Cowboy know that I did miss him, without over-doing any emotional guilt trip, and "ya" was more down-home, country, friendly—something an old pal might say.

"Well, God damn, how the hell did you know to find me here?" he asked happy, but curious.

"Just asked around, ya know?" I said, and quickly changed the subject. "How've you been, Dad?"

I wanted to keep my sentences short and to the point so that would allow more time for me to hear his voice, hear about his life. I missed Dad so much. I didn't want the Cowboy to know that though.

"Jus' been tryin' to find ranchin' work and tryin' to stay above water I reckon," and then he chuckled a bit.

"I did get in a fight at the bar about a week ago," he offered with pride and a coughing chuckle.

With no judgment, I said, "Oh yeah?"

"Some cowboy was mouthin' off and jus' started a-swingin'— got a pretty big fat lip," he admitted.

"How ya doin' in California?" he asked, quick transition.

"I'm good Dad; just working." I wanted to keep it simple, nothing to trigger worry on his part.

"Well, I best get off this phone; it's the bar phone."

"Okay, well, it was good talking with ya Dad! I'll call you again—the bartender said it was fine."

That's what I said, but I was thinking and feeling desperately, no, wait…can we talk just a little while longer?

"I love ya, will talk with ya soon."

I wanted to make sure I said those words to him; I hadn't said "I love you" to Dad in many years.

He returned the sentiment with the same fearful awkwardness that made us both vulnerable, and the conversation faded. As he said goodbye, I *could* hear tears in his goodbye. That was unusual and unexpected. I saved my tears until I hung up.

I took a deep breath; I had eight whole minutes—to talk and to listen.

———◆———

This conversation was the beginning of our almost one-year reconnection and understanding of one another through our pauses and our voices. In the beginning, I called the Buckhorn Bar every week, always before 3:00 p.m. Our afternoon chats were my favorite pastimes and I anticipated each call more and more. The bartender came to know my voice; "It's your daughter," he would say, after only a "Hello" on my end.

I could hear him handing the phone to the Cowboy at the bar. The conversations were always short. The Cowboy and I had mostly sober conversations. A couple of times, I missed the 3:00 deadline, and the Cowboy was indeed blitzed—those conversations were even shorter. "I'll call ya later Dad," followed by a click.

I tried not to let those few calls get me down; I knew what I was dealing with, I knew he was an alcoholic and the bartender warned me—and when a bartender tells you something about one of his loyal patrons, you better believe.

The sober phone conversations on the Buckhorn Bar phone though, the ones before 3:00, we had for a few months. I could see a sweet smile on his face, sitting on bar stool, talking on the phone—his hat hanging on the back of the stool, his hair thick and brown with a wave in the front partnered with a side part and a button up shirt, jeans and boots, all leaning into the bar as he talked.

Kiley's breast cancer was one of the first things I told Dad about in our conversations. That spring of 2009, after a few months of keeping my secret conversations with the Cowboy to myself, I told Kiley about talking with my Dad.

Dad wanted to know everything about her family, her kids, and what the prognosis was; it looked hopeful. She had already had a double mastectomy earlier that fall and had started chemotherapy.

Always with vulnerable sadness in his voice, the Cowboy asked about Kiley every phone conversation. I would give the updates and for the first time, felt safe enough emotionally to cry. It was only over the phone, but Dad was there comforting me as I cried for my best friend. This was a new experience for the Cowboy and I and that felt good—I'd never allowed myself to need the Cowboy in that way. Strangely, the topic of Kiley's cancer opened our hearts for more and more honest and loving conversations over the phone, as if we were sitting on a porch somewhere, drinking coffee and just catching up.

Kiley had just turned 33 that March when I went to Colorado to visit.

"Hey Ki, do you think I should go visit my Dad? He's been having seizures and I don't know what that means and I don't know if it's serious. What if it makes him feel worse if I see him? What if I feel worse?"

Of course I had told Kiley about the secret phone conversations with the Cowboy; she'd listen and always say, "You're just thinking about it way too much June Bug. Yes, yes you should go see him. If I could go see my dad, I would."

But, still, I didn't venture to Laramie—the Cowboy, the unknown.

The short chats gave way to our current lives, but also reminiscing about our former lives on the ranch.

My re-kindled connection with the Cowboy, even if it were just over the phone, made me think about my childhood on the ranch. Life on the ranch was one adventure and discovery after another, but it was the Cowboy's spirit and energy that brought the magic to my childhood. Memories were what I had left of the Cowboy and the ranch, so I learned to live in them, soaking up and absorbing each recollection like water in an irrigation ditch.

I shoved the assignment in my backpack and moped on the bus ride home. I was eight years old—I remember two things from the 2nd grade: learning cursive and writing swirly letters between the wide, blue lines on the notebook paper, and a music instrument project of all things.

The bus driver, Mrs. Stewart, noticed my cranky stomp up the bus steps and asked, "Rough day Melissa?" Mrs. Stewart was in her 60s, short grayish hair with a slight violet tint, and knew all of the kids' names, as any good bus driver would in a small town. She always wore bright pink lipstick and seemed quite sophisticated for a bus driver; she was more like a sweet, wise, sassy grandmother. I zoned out, gazing at the fields as the bus drove along the Seven-Mile Road. I knew many of my fellow classmates would make shoe-box guitars with rubber bands; I needed something grander. I got off the bus and dragged myself down the dirt road toward the house, thinking.

Just before bed, kissing my parents goodnight, Mom said, "You have a music assignment for school—what do you want to make?"

"Something *big*," I said.

The next morning over the usual scrambled eggs breakfast, Dad came in for his breakfast and coffee. The Cowboy had already been out working since 5:00 am feeding the cattle. During the winter months, the snow was deep, and Dad and his ranch hand used two draft horses harnessed to a rather large wooden wagon filled with hay. The Cowboy, often with icicles hanging on to his mustache, walked in the porch, stomped the snow off his boots and was carrying a metal pipe: about four feet long and two inches wide at the opening.

"This is your instrument!" he said. He seemed really excited about my 2nd grade music project. I was, well, skeptical of the pipe.

"After school today come into the shop and we'll get started."

That night, we constructed the most perfect musical instrument—a harp! No one else would have an instrument like mine! Dad welded and shaped the pipe into a half circle and we tied fishing line from one end of the pipe to the other for the strings. As a finishing touch, I spray-painted the pipe silver.

It didn't make beautiful music, but it sure looked like it did. Standing just about as tall as me, I lugged my harp onto the bus, carrying a big smile.

"Whatcha got there?" asked Mrs. Stewart.

"A harp...for my assignment!" I said, with snooty pride and a smile.

Trying not to ruin my enthusiasm, and yet still being concerned for the safety of others with this monstrosity on the bus, she sweetly said: "Just put it under the seat in front of you, Hun."

Fourteen

I indulged in every word the Cowboy spoke. He sat at the bar, on the phone as I studied his words, his tone and his stories. As an adult child of an alcoholic I was trained to seek and understand the minutest communication and descramble it. I was an expert at it; hell, I should have worked for the FBI or CIA as an interrogator, sensing and observing even the slightest mistruth and manipulation.

Adult children of alcoholics—our instincts are keenly precise; we rely on this to survive our brokenness. After a few months, the Cowboy revealed he had a "gal" friend whom he now lived with in a trailer-home. I kept my judgments and worries to myself; at least he had shelter. He also offered a phone number; it was a number I could ring instead of the Buckhorn. This meant that our conversations could be longer than five minutes and that was a welcomed, happy realization.

Our conversations over the months got more lighthearted and comfortable although I was still keenly aware of the fragility of my heart and his disease. I was usually lounging at home or driving on my way to work on the 101, catching a moment to chat with Dad with the ocean view.

"So how is your drinking?" was like asking, "So how are you?" I asked both questions often, and without hesitation, and he answered truthfully: "I don't really have bad days; some days are just better than others."

"When do I get to be a grandpa?"

"Good question Dad," I laughed and changed the subject.

———◆———

The truth was I had all sorts of dating dilemmas and stories— funny stories about my singlehood involving everything from being on the Bachelor reality show twice –in retrospect, thank God I didn't make it past the second taping, to an Oprah episode with Steve Harvey on being single ... oh that's a good story! Kiley got to hear about each one, imitations and re-enactments and all—in fact it was how we passed the time from the moment she picked me up at the airport in Denver, all the way back to Del Norte – a four-hour drive full of hysterics. Kiley's mom and sister—Ann and Lisa—were often with Kiley to pick me up. "Tell us again about the weatherman with the Southern accent!" They started laughing before I could even re-tell the story. "I'd like you to read this" a counselor I saw *once* at the private Christian university I attended for graduate school. I told him about the one-night stand with a man I had only known a day; he was Italian-Spanish. After about 20 minutes in our first session, he handed me a book titled, "Women, Sex and Addiction". "You think I'm a sex addict?" I said surprised and worried. He stumbled and seemed to speak his thoughts out loud, "No, no, that's not exactly what I meant ...I knew it was too soon to bring it up." "Yu-think?" I thought later; at the moment though I took the book with the intention of reading it. It's sitting on my bookshelf now if someone would like to borrow it. Another counselor (female) and close girlfriends said I had just done what they all had in their undergrad years; those were the years I was hitched. Still, in the ten years or so after my divorce I had a few long-term relationships, but the "seriousness" of the commitment didn't necessarily translate into healthy. In between, I dated *Dick and Jane* style, but the older I got, the more boring that became. A one-night stand with a mostly straight girl … I don't remember her name—oh that was a first … Kiley had to talk me down from my hysteria about it—"Boobs, big boobs, no-no-no-no" I squirmed as I recounted. She was calm, "June, it's called experimentation—ya tried it, ya didn't like it and now ya know." I had an affair with a married man, who, of course needed to keep me a secret—we made out on the dark beach, *but*, he was already separated after all and the divorce just hadn't been finalized yet. The shame was building. I'd had a glass of wine with a nice fella it seemed; he was a paramedic and we'd met through acquaintances. I sipped my wine as we sat at a table with a group of his friends, a couple of them police officers and firemen. That was the last thing I remember—I woke up in my apartment and had no idea how I'd gotten there and I had no idea where my car was either. The shame was enormous. By the time I was mid-30's, I knew something had to shift. So I dated a musician ten years younger than me.

"Dang it June bug, we were supposed to have kids at the same time; I'll be a grandma by the time you have kids," Kiley used to say to me. I didn't have the marriage and the kids, but I had my education, teaching and life in Santa Barbara. These brought some balance and joy into my life; they filled most of the void I felt from losing my family and the home where I grew up. Love—the truest and deepest kind, in the form of a male companion—was the only thing I couldn't seem to wrangle.

———◆———

Although I didn't tell Dad everything, I did tell him how I felt about me and him—and the honesty and openness of our conversations was refreshing to both of us. He asked about Mom and some days his questions flared with hints of anger, resentment, "How's your mother?" Before I could answer, "Never mind, I could give a shit about her and that husband of hers."

But as our conversations went on, the same question would come up and it was me who wanted to avoid it because I could hear the sort of "love of your life" emotion behind the question. So when he asked, "How's your mom doing?" I paused, conscious of his real desire to know.

"She's good Dad. She's happy," I said with such certainty, wanting to convey I wasn't just saying it to make him feel good.

Our questions and answers were like the gentle tide rolling on the beach and back into the ocean; it was the view from the 101 that I had been looking for. The Cowboy was really never forthright about his health or alcoholism, until now. I could just sense he was telling the truth and I think he felt, finally, that he could just tell me what was going on. It certainly was different than from when I was a teenager when traces of the disease—a trail of empty beer cans—tipped me off of his whereabouts. Back then it was the same puzzle that I learned to piece together over and over.

Like when I was sixteen and zipping down the dirt road in my 83 Ford Escort, I created a dusty trail. There was no use in ever washing my car really. In the distance, perhaps a half mile away past the sawbuck fences and hay bales, I saw what seemed to be a still image. I slowed the car down and thought, "Now, what the hell...?"

I squinted and noticed it was the tractor stopped in the middle of the field. It seemed odd and I looked closer—the Cowboy was just sitting there, doing nothing, and something seemed strange about his posture, the outline of the shape. Instead of continuing toward the ranch house, I turned onto the barely noticeable little road which nature had been trying to reclaim, and drove toward the still frame. I scrunched forward and as I got closer. "Oh, God damn it!" I said when I realized the Cowboy had passed out over the wheel of the tractor, with empty beer cans scattered around the tractor.

I stomped over to the John Deer and hopped on the tractor; "Dad? Dad ... Dad!" I said, poking him in the shoulder the whole time.

One side of his face was sunburned; he must have been out there for a couple of hours. He lifted his head up, cowboy hat tilted to the side—he was shit-faced, and I could smell the alcohol as his hunched over body tried to sit up straight.

"Nap time huh?" I said, pissed. I wasn't always like that—only times when I found him in situations where he could have gotten himself killed.

"Coooome on, let's get ya home." I softened up.

"Naaa, I'm gonna stay here," he blubbered. "Be home in a little while."

"Ooookay. Fine!" I pouted, and left him there.

But now, on the phone, we weren't bargaining anymore. We had reached a candid place in our connection, where the Cowboy was honest—not guilt ridden—and explained things just as they were.

"I enjoy a beer or two with my buddy Dave," Dad offered when I would ask him about his drinking.

Dave was a drinking buddy, but it seemed they looked out for each other, probably in an "outlaw" sort of way, but nonetheless, I heard a smile when Dad talked about hanging out with Dave at the Buckhorn Bar. Miles away and only via phone, I heard and sensed a different type of healing. The physical signs of illness were still there—I heard the Cowboy coughing more than usual and it was different than the slight smoker's cough he'd had for years. It was more of a wheezing.

"Oh, think I got another cold," he'd offer, seemingly unworried.

Late spring and summer brought more concern, a gut feeling so deep that it knocked the wind out of me, like I'd just been just kicked by a horse.

"I've been kinda sick lately," Dad admitted, hesitantly. "Had a seizure 'couple days back—using a cane now to help me walk, get in and out of bed."

"Seizures? What? Why? Are you sure? Have you gone to a doctor?" I asked.

The Cowboy explained that he had been to a community clinic a handful of times for the seizures; they gave him anti-seizure medication. This scared the hell out of me, but what scared me even more was my intuition that *he* was worried.

I recalled the time the Cowboy picked me up after school when he had been drinking. I had control; I drove us home.

With each phone conversation, Dad shared that the seizures were getting worse; after a conversation would end, I grasped my hands in a fist, lightly pounding my head as to trigger an answer: "What the hell is going on…what do I do, what do I do?"

More than ever I contemplated visiting him—why was I so afraid of going? I needed to get past my emotional boundary police so that I could make a decision.

It was a labyrinth of this way or that way and I got lost, paralyzed with the contemplation. The fear had a tight grip on both my emotional and rational sides and held me back from visiting him. My longing to visit him collided with the emotional shootout I envisioned and each rationalization—my teaching schedule, my limited budget—was a bullet I dodged. What really frightened me was what I would see, and even worse feel, if I visited the Cowboy. I rehearsed the scene—fly into Denver, rent a car and take a lonely drive to Laramie Wyoming, allowing three hours to consider what I was getting into. Skeptically, I'd coast into the trailer park, armed with my stockpile of emotional weapons, and look for Dad. I was afraid that the moment I saw him I was a goner—to see him walking with a cane, half of his body limp from the seizure he described, his sidekick an old haint holding whiskey. All of it a smoking gun revealing just how broken we were.

Every letter and call was bitter sweet—indulging in his voice, laugh and hearing him listen to me; that was *the* most beautiful sound. But with every word he'd written or spoken, I heard another whisper: "Go."

———◆———

Fifteen

He followed everything with, "I'll be damn."
That's what the Cowboy always said when I told him about one of my adventures, like living in Italy for three months when I was thirty-two, or accomplishments like finishing graduate school or having a story published. These life goals served me well, but they were another way I thought I could outrun his alcoholism and protect myself with a cloak of education and success.

There was never a conversation that Dad didn't talk about his dreams and goals too—Cowboy dreams.

"I reckon when I get back on my feet I can get a-horse, saddle and a-few cattle and maybe even have my own small outfit someday."

"Ya that would be good for ya Dad," I said with certainty and encouragement.

Years before he'd still had dreams of the rodeo. "I figure I just need a truck and trailer to haul Paint. I just need to practice." Paint was his roping horse. Now, though, he no longer talked about the rodeo, only ranching.

Our conversations got intense when he talked about the woman he lived with. She was mean—I often heard her yelling in the background. It didn't surprise me that she, too, was an alcoholic. When I called she always answered the phone.

"Is my Dad there?" I asked as nicely as possible, but I gritted my teeth at even the thought of being on the phone with *her* for even a second.

"HUUUUH?" she said with a drunk hic-cup.

By then Dad just grabbed the phone, "Yaeeeeeaalow" he said in a funny way like always.

The dusty town of Laramie, with the Buckhorn Bar down a side street and the trailer park the Cowboy and the woman lived in—I imagined their trailer, old, small and hoisted up on cement bricks. When I thought about visiting the Cowboy, I tried to envision the situation: there would probably be an old truck parked outside; maybe it would start and maybe it wouldn't. Inside Dad would be relaxing in a worn, comfortable recliner, his only oasis they got at a thrift store. I was sure it was a narrow trailer from the 60s, and it reeked of cigarette smoke. It was an ugly place of temptation for a Cowboy full of wavering hope and little resistance to his addiction.

At the beginning of summer, I received in the mail a short note from the Cowboy.

Melissa,
    I just have time for a few lines. I hope Kiley is better.
We went to a church picnic yesterday. I am supposed to go
to a healing prayer meeting today. I love you.
Dad

The familiar cursive, creative handwriting he'd once had was shaky now, and that made me study the words longer, as if the answer to what caused the shakes would reveal itself—was it withdrawal? Or something else? The Cowboy took the time, as he says, "...for a few lines." Still, to get a short note, scribbled, mailed and an "I love you" was a gift, a love note that I posted on my refrigerator so I could see it every day.

"What is the last thing you remember right before you have a seizure?"

Another call and another seizure; Dad had just gotten home from the hospital. I rationalized that the Cowboy must not be too bad if they sent him home with just more medication. Still, what the hell was causing the seizures?

I was determined to figure out this mystery. "Dad, really think about it. What's the last thing you remember right before a seizure?"

There was a brief silence as Dad thought through what happened in those seconds before he convulsed so badly that he couldn't remember anything. And then he said it; he gave his answer slowly as if he finally realized the reason as he spoke each word.

"Well ... I remember that just before every seizure I have had, I am sober. And I'm thinking of all of the things I have done wrong and the people I have lost, mostly the lost time with you kids and your mother. Ya, that's what I remember just before a seizure happens."

I was expecting to hear more physical reasons—light-headedness, sick to the stomach, headache. The Cowboy choked up a bit trailing that last word and I grasped my chest as if I could grab my heart and hold it together; I dropped my head and cried.

"Dad, do you remember those farmers you got my kitten from?"

I wanted him to know that I hadn't forgotten anything that he ever gave me.

I was along for a ride with Dad in the ranch truck. He had business to do with a farmer; most of Dad's connections were with fellow ranchers—horse and cattle ranches, not pigs and chickens as the Cowboy proudly explained to me one day. "I am a rancher, not a farmer. Cowboys are ranchers and farmers have pigs and chickens." I never forgot that lesson—my dad: the Cowboy, the Rancher.

We drove on dirt roads for a long time to finally arrive at a place deep in the country. It was filthy and the house had been constructed with plywood and the stables around were full of, sure enough, pigs and chickens; they were clearly *farmers*. Dad told me to wait in the truck and later I would hear him telling Mom about how there was no electricity there, how the family of seven lived in filth, and the five kids were home-schooled. I sat in the truck waiting for the Cowboy and noticed one of the farmer boys in the stables—he had greasy hair, a dirty face. Dad waved for me to get out of the truck— I hesitated, but it seemed he had something to show me. "Come on, hurry up Melissa," he said with a stern, but eager tone. Dad saw something he knew I would love—kittens!

The farmers raised Persian cats and sold them for several hundred dollars. They were the cutest things I had ever seen—flat-as-a-pancake faces, and fluffy as can be— but I could see they were not really taken care of. They were sickly and meowed in a wailing sort of way, almost to say "Pleeeeease take me (away from these farmers) and take care of me."

The Cowboy and I headed back home and all I could think of was that adorable deep-gray-with-a-blue-hue, extremely fluffy, flat-faced and boogied copper-eyed kitten. I didn't know they were $500, I just knew I wanted the fluffy one. The Cowboy, too, wanted me to have what I wanted. Mom and Dad must have discussed it because we went back to that farmer and I picked out a kitten—the blue Persian with copper eyes. As I sat there playing with my new kitten, I was completely occupied and forgot about the bad smell in the plywood house. I noticed, though, that the Cowboy was making a deal with the farmer; Dad certainly didn't have $500 so he handed the farmer a pair of chaps.

"How about these? Now these are nearly brand new, worth more than $500," the Cowboy negotiated for a fluff ball. Chaps for a Persian cat; my Cowboy Dad traded his chaps for a kitten, for me. On the way home, I held the little kitten tight and named him "Blue".

I had Blue for ten years.

"I love you Dad," I said now, very intentionally at the end of every call.

"I love you too, Hun."

I always waited to hear the click on the other end before I hung up the phone. I seemed to debrief myself after each conversation, considering all that was said and thinking about the effects of alcohol on my Cowboy Dad and on me.

I certainly knew Dad's drinking was a coping mechanism of sorts; it lightened the harshness of the reality of his bad choices and worse consequences. Alcohol offered temporary solace and forgetfulness and actually gave a slight dose of happiness to Dad. If sadness and regret were so deep as to cause a physical tremor or seizure of the body, then how could Dad resist the brief numbing of his fix?

The genuine promises, good intentions and a sincere desire to be and do better— these thoughts, words and actions of an addict are heart-breaking to, yes, the people around them, but also for the person with the addiction. These are not empty promises or vindictive actions; they are true desires and when their disease lets others and themselves down (again and again), it's devastating to their spirit. And so the addiction wins again with another hit. It's like getting your tractor stuck in the mud. You keep grinding the gears, but the mud is too thick—too deep—and the tires are too worn to grip the ground

I received another letter received just a couple of weeks later in July 2009; I just turned thirty-four years old:

> Melissa,
>   Just a few lines to wish you a happy birthday. Are you going to do something? The doctor took me off my medications. I guess that means I'm better. I am still a little shaky. Well, that's about all for now.
>   I love you. Dad

Shaky handwriting and another letter—despite being taken off medications, I started to worry more. Dad hadn't sent me birthday wishes in several years; I learned to know this was not because he didn't love me or because he didn't remember my birthday—that is the very reason he *didn't* connect.

I still thought about visiting the Cowboy as his letters and words hinted something to me I wouldn't hear.

———◆———

Kiley was still receiving chemotherapy treatments and I ventured to Colorado again at the end of July. I went along with her to the Alamosa hospital for a routine treatment. Kiley seemed quite used to and acclimated in the clinical environment which used a homey décor to soften the stiffness of a room with hospital beds, IVs and the sterile smell.

"Hello ladies!" Kiley said in her cheerful and sassy way to the nurses as we walked into the room with a couple of cancer patients getting their treatments. Of course, she wasn't thrilled to have the re-occurring treatment that made her moan in agony, but she was sincerely optimistic and it showed in the littlest details of her life—how she didn't allow it to completely disrupt her daily *living*. Kiley still coached volleyball and went to work every day as a social worker to be an advocate for children. Kiley was still Kiley—only she had a bald head covered with a different, beautiful scarf every day. A mom, wife, sister, daughter and best friend—she loved each role genuinely and continued indulging in each one.

I followed her into the treatment room reserved for her that day; I was right behind her, following her every move. I didn't realize it at the time, but I was anxious and scared—this was a territory that was not familiar to me and as I could feel the terror, I tried to play it cool.

Kiley got comfortable in a bed sitting upright and the nurse started the treatment; in that moment, I could feel the color leave my face.

I was about to cry uncontrollably; it wasn't the hospital bed or IVs, it was that question that hadn't seemed real up until this point: *Kiley could actually die.*

I could not let Kiley see me like this; she was the one after all who needed looking after. So I said—normal voice, no quiver—"I have to pee so bad...where's the restroom?"

Kiley pointed behind me, "You can go in there June bug."

I rushed in without looking like I was taking cover. I just stood in the dark at first with my back against the wall; I knew I couldn't cry because she would see my puffy, red eyes. I took several breaths to try to keep in the tears and yet some still escaped. My shaky hand flipped the light on and I held myself steady and over the sink.

I gazed in the mirror. *Kiley has breast cancer,* I thought.

I splashed cold water on my face to wash away the realization. Up until that moment in that room with Kiley, I couldn't believe she was actually sick. What a terrible time to have this conversation with myself, but was there really a *good* time?

Turbulence rolled around in my chest, looking for an escape. I'd been in the restroom for several minutes; I flushed the toilet and turned the sink water on again.

"You okay in there?" Kiley raised her voice to reach me in the bathroom.

"Oh, yeah," I answered nonchalantly as I opened the door.

"I figured ya fell in the toilet! Well, come up here and lay with me June bug," she said, patting the bed.

And so we snuggled, talked and she played with my hair; we laid there for a couple of hours and every so often she would reach out her arm for the waste basket to vomit in, and I would lean over and get it for her.

As Kiley dozed off, I covered us in the quilt she brought from home and daydreamed about our friendship through the years. Visiting the abandoned Flying W Ranch was something I did every time I would visit the San Luis Valley. Kiley and I were planning to go together tomorrow, the day after her chemo. But in my mind, I was already there.

———•———

Just about half a mile past the ranch houses, on the dirt road and along the saw buck fences, stood an old rickety house—a shop perhaps where wood work was done, long ago—and an old barn. In those childhood summers on the ranch, those old wooden buildings made all of us who played there—me, Kiley, and my brother and his friends— feel like we were on a treasure hunt, discovering old newspapers, bottles, and other interesting junk. In reality, nothing was really that old—newspapers were from the 60s, and the house had been rummaged through before we had even moved to the Flying W. The first summer that we found the "old barns" as we called them collectively, Kiley and I were young enough to want to hold hands as we walked down the dirt road to get there, passing the lake where we would catch minnows and put them in a jar and later wonder why they floated to the top.

"Watch out for the rattlers, especially under 'em floor boards in the old barns," Dad would always remind.

"We got the snakebite kit," we'd assure him.

Crazy thing is, in the heat of the Colorado summer, under the broken-up porch floor at the old barns was pretty much a rattle-snake haven. Thinking back, Dad had to have known that, but he never stopped us from our summer adventures.

Kiley and I played mostly in the old house, "This room is the kitchen ... and this will be the living room ... and this is my bedroom," Kiley would say, running to each room. We'd imagine where we would put furniture and when we would have friends over. Standing in the spot I'd chosen, "How about a couch here, and the kitchen table about here." I'd scramble to that spot in front of a window in the kitchen, where we had a view of the old barn. The old shop had old license plates nailed to the walls, which kept our attention for a few minutes one afternoon, but it was dark and shady, which meant spiders and they were scarier than any snake. The (actual) old barn was a small barn, with dry old hay scattered around and molded to the old wood fixtures. What made the old barn interesting though, were the meows of wild kittens; we saw the mother cat running around, but could never find where she had those kittens hidden. And so Kiley and I would play all afternoon in the old house with nothing but our little-girl imaginations.

The end of the season was the hottest in the Valley and definitely on the ranch. One day, the sun slipped through the old barn roof and caught the glance of a piece of bottle glass; the glass basking in the sun, surrounded by dry hay, caught fire. The old barn was in flames! The Cowboy was on the tractor in a nearby pasture and saw the smoke right away. Someone from the houses had already called the volunteer firemen, and Dad, thinking that we were playing in the old barns—we weren't that day—drove the truck quickly to the fire. Moments later, the Cowboy walked into the house, still wearing his cowboy hat; his jeans and boots were covered in soot. His sweaty face was black from the smoke, and in his arms, held close to his chest, was a scared, striped cat with singed hair and ear. The Cowboy, hearing a desperate meow, rescued the mother cat; she had been wild and fending for herself and her kittens just fine with the plentiful mice in the old barns.

The fire truck had arrived and put out the fire, which luckily only burned the old barn and hay, not the other old buildings—although the loss was felt by us kids.

And for the next ten years, the mother cat was wild no more; she was known as "mama cat" and was loyal to the Cowboy—being a good mouser around our home and always seeking a scratch under the chin by any one of us, but mainly the guy wearing the hat. Turns out too that mama cat had those kittens hidden under the porch of the old house, and they had been old enough to fend for themselves when the fire broke. A few weeks later we had four more wild cats running around that we would catch a glimpse of.

And every summer after that, even through high school, Kiley and I would ride our bikes by the old barns, just because.

Sixteen

I went home to California, escaping another excuse not to visit the Cowboy in Wyoming—although I told him all about my visit to see Kiley and the ranch.

"She's had some headaches lately, but she's always had migraines. She's good Dad, really good and she told me to tell you 'hi'!"

That week I drove to work from Santa Barbara to Ventura along the 101 South. The ocean to my right was calming, which I needed more than I realized. My trips to Colorado and visits to the ranch gave me vivid memories of Kiley and me and our silly snake adventures and the Cowboy right alongside. And especially after this last trip, I realized that Kiley was getting better, but *still* had *cancer*.

I was driving in a trance—all of these thoughts swirling around my mind—when on the radio I heard those familiar guitar chords first, then the lyrics: "You just call out my name, and you know wherever I am, I'll come runnin' to see you again."

I dialed Kiley and when she answered, "Hey Junebug!" I turned up the radio and started singing to her: "Winter, spring, summer, or fall, all you have to do is call and I'll be there, yeah, yeah, yeah, you've got a friend."

She sang along too, the next line, "If the sky above you should turn dark and full of clouds ..." Then we both giggled through the next line—we weren't sure of the lyrics— and then harmoniously picked up the next chorus: "keep your head together and call my name out loud."

Meanwhile, Kiley's headaches continued.

One day, when she wasn't answering, I called her husband. "Why isn't she answering her cell? What's going on?" I asked him.

"Just get here as soon as you can."

———◆———

I was on a plane again to Colorado. I stared out the window, gazing at the clouds and questioning for the first time if there really was a heaven. I heard no other sounds around me except my own thoughts. I needed to get there in time. Would I get there in time?

Kiley was unconscious when I arrived. Just two months earlier, we'd been sipping cherry limeades at Sonic and laughing. Now I stared at my best friend, whose hair and eyebrows had turned to a stark grey and white. She had the cutest button nose—she got it from her mom; I had always wanted her nose and her round face. Her skin was pale, but revealed a bit of pink tone.

The young doctor's grave concern showed in the tension in his brows and his shaky voice, searching for words. "Kiley's pain is beyond what we can comprehend. My staff and I are devastated. In all my years of treating cancer patients, I have never seen such an aggressive cancer in someone so young. I'm so sorry, but there is nothing else we can do; it's not a matter of days, it's really a matter of hours." The doctor held steady in his delivery of the news, but I could see his sadness and defeat, as if he'd been avoiding this conclusion.

I laid my head next to her on the bed; she was barely conscious and through the night felt her lift her arm and gently stroke my hair with just the pads of her fingers—it was a light pat, not moving her fingers. The physical movement of her fingers through my hair, lifting it from the roots, was not there—not like it was just a few weeks before when we were together. But I could feel, deeply, the spiritual energy transferred from her to me. I could feel that she knew I was there and experiencing an agony I had never felt before. I could feel my heart as if it were more than an organ, more like its own living, emotional being inside me—it was a warm sensation surrounding my heart and lungs, pulsing and spreading as I soaked the blanket with my tears. I laid there in disbelief that there was no hope, no miracle and that my best friend would be gone very soon. I stayed through the night and dreaded the morning when I would have to pull myself away from her.

The next day, I was so paralyzed, I could hardly walk. I sat down on the bed, held her familiar hand—I grazed her hand with mine, noticing familiar scars and traits of her hands. Kiley was in and out of consciousness, which seemed a conscious effort to *be in* these final moments on earth with each person who loved her so. I stroked her forehead and traced the outline of her face with my fingers, hoping that in some way a part of her spirit would transfer, enter me, stay with me and never leave.

With both of my warm palms I felt her soft, grey hair and then cradled her face in my hands. "I love you Kiley, my best friend," I wept.

I wanted to say "You will be okay" and "I'll miss you," but I hesitated, thinking, is that too final? Maybe there will be a miracle in the coming hours and she will not die? That thinking lasted only half a second and I realized this was the end and my final good bye.

I needed to not be afraid and I needed to say what I realized Kiley also knew—that she would die and these were the last words that I would be privileged to say to my best friend.

"Kiley, you will always be my best friend. You will be okay."

And I meant that she would be okay—that even with death she would be okay. And so I spoke those words too: "Don't be afraid Kiley" and I said them with a steady, confident voice so she could hear my certainty. All the words and feelings I spoke were so final and with every word, that finality sounded strange and unfamiliar. I had never said goodbye to someone, let alone my best friend, knowing that they would be gone forever. But we both knew this was our last best friend conversation, and what needed to be conveyed was truth—and love.

My whole body and spirit were not mine; they seemed to just be a mobile hanging above Kiley's bed, trying to nurture her. With just the little energy she had, Kiley pried her eyes open and with a look of true love, mumbled: "Don't cry, June bug."

My heart sank into her words and we locked eyes for just a few wonderful seconds. Then her eyelids were like a sunset, meeting the horizon to rest. I whispered my last words to her, "I will miss you Kiley."

I pulled myself away from her, battling my urge to stay and cling to her arm. I knew it was the last time I would ever see her alive – what a surreal message surging through my mind and body—that I would never see Kiley again on this earth.

———◆———

I waited a day to reveal the incomprehensible—that an angry cancer took away a beautiful, young, mother, daughter, sister and best friend. I dialed each number slowly as I contemplated how I would tell Dad the news. It seemed backward—telling Dad of Kiley's death; I always thought that it would be the other way around. Of course in my denial, the story in my mind was something closer to Kiley being healed and cured, the two of us living long lives and she wrapping her old frail arms around me when the Cowboy died at a lucky old age from stubborn alcoholism.

Kiley and I once overheard her eleven-year-old daughter, Josie, tell her friend at her birthday slumber party, "Umm...yaaa, my mom and Melissa have been friends like forever and they know eeeeverything about each other." Josie had heard the stories and she loved them; Kiley and I were certain that by the time Jo was a teenager she would be completing the story for us and saying, "not that story again" and rolling her eyes as teenagers do.

Kiley knew me better than I knew myself. I remember when my ex-husband revealed on the phone that he'd been having an affair. I'd basically pushed him to just say it. Although I wasn't in love with him anymore, and had "mentally" cheated on him, too— with a co-worker I had a crush on—I wasn't prepared for the end, couldn't fathom him being intimate with someone else. We were high school sweethearts, first and only loves. So I ran, literally, for miles. I'm not a runner—I take leisurely walks and hikes and if you saw me, I would probably be stopping to literally smell the roses (or jasmine) or pick up a shell on the beach. But that day, I ran as fast as I could along a path that lead to an open meadow. My chest didn't hurt, I wasn't out of breath, and I couldn't feel my legs; somebody else was running for me. I couldn't stop, so I ran to the next park a few miles away. I stood at the end of the path, my head spinning. I looked down and realized I had no shoes on. I wiggled my toes in the dirty white cotton that covered my feet.

Finally, I landed on Kiley's couch. I still remember what she said.

"Well, he's an idiot ya know? He'll regret it," Kiley said to gage my emotions.

"Do you really want to be with him June bug? You've been unhappy." She tactfully pointed out the forgotten obvious, like only a true friend can do.

———◆———

"Hi Dad," I said with a low voice, paused, then continued. "Well, Dad … Kiley didn't make it and passed away yesterday."

I held my breath, got the bad news out and then I breathed and cried.

The Cowboy sobbed when I told him that Kiley passed away; he was not expecting this news. I *heard* and *felt* a two-second hesitation of disbelief, and then I heard the sorrow in his inability to console me.

He choked a bit as if to hold in the cry, took a breath and said, "Ohh, I'm … I'm so sorry Honey." Then Dad wept *with* me for the first time in my life, for the loss that we both felt.

I had never heard or seen the Cowboy—or any cowboy for that matter—cry, not even when they were bucked off in a rodeo, losing the great buckle or prize. When I was little, I had always asked Dad when I saw the other cowboys lose their competition or get bucked off, "Is he going to cry?" Dad assured me, with a chuckle, "Cowboys don't cry," and rubbed the top of my head, gave a wink and clicked his tongue.

The Cowboy shared my sadness for Kiley, but his came more from knowing mine. It's a grief that just takes time to not hurt as much, but there wasn't a single thing that was offered or told to me that made it go away, until the Cowboy told me a story.

"Do you remember the fawn?" Dad offered gently.

"The fawn?" I asked with a slight, subconscious hint of remembrance, though I had no idea what he was referencing.

I sensed that there was a precious memory locked away and I could feel the return of it. It's as if the Cowboy had this memory stored away for the saddest of days for his Melissa.

"You don't remember?" he asked. "Well," he started, and I could hear the lump in his throat. "You were about ten years old. It was in the early morning and you were still fast asleep." This painted a picture in my mind; I was there, sleeping soundly in my bed as the light of the sunrise trickled through the pine trees outside of my bedroom windows.

"I was on the swather that morning and the alfalfa was tall. As I sectioned cutting, row by row, I noticed a baby deer—a fawn, jus' lying there in a pocket of the tall alfalfa, without his momma. I stopped the swather, hopped out and took hold of him with both of my arms. I mean, I knew he was scared by the sounds of the large machine that was cutting down the hiding place his momma had made for him."

The memory was slowly trickling back as I held the phone to my ear.

"I carried the little guy to the truck and drove back to the house; that's when I carried him into your bedroom and took him to your bedside."

The memory was starting to rush back. "Oh! Ya, I *do* remember that," I said. "Keep going."

"I kneeled at your bedside, holding the brown fawn with white spots, 'Melissa ... Melissa ... wake up Honey.'

I remembered opening my eyes and seeing the Cowboy with his hat still on and kneeling with a baby deer in his arms; I was so delighted!

The Cowboy still had his leather gloves on; "Look what I found this morning, lying all by himself," the Cowboy whispered.

The memory rushed back to me like a savior. My Cowboy Dad kneeling at my bedside—his golden mustache, his careful demeanor and sound and smell of his leather chaps and gloves in his movements to hold the fawn carefully. I'd thought I was in a dream, and then realized quickly that I was not; I just wanted to touch this baby dear.

"Be real still and don't touch him because his momma will smell your scent."

My Cowboy kneeled by my bedside and held this fawn in his arms. I was a half asleep and mesmerized; it was like I was in a fairytale.

The fawn was a light, cinnamon brown with dainty white spots here and there; his piercing brown eyes stared at me with a slight, but trusting uncertainty, and his little black nose seemed to breathe calmly despite being in my bedroom that morning. His long ears that twitched just a bit. His delicate legs, so tiny.

After a few minutes, Dad said, "Well, better get the little fella back to his momma before she gets too worried."

I gave the precious creature one more awe-stare and tried to hold the glance and then drifted back to sleep—and kept it in a dream bank for 24 years. I didn't remember the morning fawn until the Cowboy shared the story with me and, for a few minutes, it took my mind completely away from my grief.

Seventeen

A s Dad continued to talk about living his dreams, I thought about how he had already done so. A horse, saddle, truck and a dog are the foundational desires of any cowboy. A cowboy though, always wants to work the ranch, ride and rodeo. Dad never had his own land, but his work on the ranch made it seem like his own. Irrigating, calving, dragging the fields, bailing hay, and building fences loaned an earned sense of ownership. The Cowboy knew, in his heart, that it was *his* hands that worked the ranch. Unlike his legs that never saw the light of day because he wore long johns, jeans and boots all year, his strong, hard-working hands were tan and tough.

I recall only once seeing him in an awkward pair of cut-off jean shorts when we went to the Great Sand Dunes. In the 80s jean shorts were in style, but the Cowboy knew nothing other than jeans, so he just cut a pair into shorts to wear for that day at the Dunes. His legs and feet were a milky white—the same color of his upper lip I saw once when he shaved off his sun-bleached mustache and his forehead, which was always shaded by his brimmed hat.

His hands though—thick-skinned, calloused and tan—revealed the hard work: using hay picks to stack hay, cinching up the saddles and working with dry, coarse braided rope. The Cowboy's hands were stocky, broad with muscle in every finger. Grease from fixing the tractors permanently filled in the grooves of his fingerprints.

At the end of a long day's work and after supper, Dad's humorous plea to me was to rub his tired hands; "Ten-ten" he would offer with a convincing smile. This meant ten seconds rubbing each hand.

I'd studied his hands; his fingers naturally curved into his palm. I tried to flatten them when I stretched and massaged his fingers and hands, but the muscle bounced back the stiffness into a slight fist. Years of holding a rope tight when riding a horse gave the Cowboy his distinctive hands and I giggled every time he sat in his recliner and asked, "Ten-ten?"

In the early years, all while I was a kid and through high school graduation—before the need for alcohol took over—the Cowboy rode his horse "Paint" in the rodeo every summer, competing in the team roping events. Saddle, spurs, chaps and a hat—all the things that lend to the cowboy spirit—paled in comparison to the Cowboy himself.

The dark, scuffed leather chaps flapped with each step toward the shoot. The faded, worn-in jeans, the cow-leather gloves and the button-up western shirt, all were nothing without the Cowboy. Dad gave wear-and-tear to the jeans, a grip of the saddle horn to the gloves, and the smell of dust and sweat to the shirt. The cowboy boots— made to weather the ranch and rodeo with every ride—and the spurs that partnered with the boots to urge the horse to go faster to catch the get-away calf.

And the cowboy hat—the felt, light grey cowboy hat that had given the Cowboy shade and was only really made his own after he killed a rattlesnake, skinned it and used it as a hat band. But even the most recognizable asset of a cowboy—the hat—was just a hat, without my dad, the Cowboy.

Even without all of that, anyone could still see he was the real deal. Even with the shade of his hat, the outdoor work of a cattleman gave a handsome, rugged quality to the Cowboy. Crow's feet etched around his eyes from smiling at the sun and from dragging the manure through the fields in the summer months his skin was tan, but surprisingly not leathered.

Dad didn't chew tobacco and his teeth were a strong-bone white with just a tad of crookedness. Cigarette smoke curled around his mustache made straw-yellow from the sun. In the winter, the mustache carried tiny icicles after feeding the cattle with the draft horses through the several feet of snow in the pastures.

My dad was the real deal.

Eighteen

"**I** promise I'll mail it this week! I love you and miss you ... bye, Dad!"

I always ended calls with Dad in an enthusiastic high pitch because I was sincerely excited that I got to hear his voice again, but also because the caretaker I had become as a child of an alcoholic knew this tone conveyed a sense that "everything will be alright".

This particular call, the Cowboy found a way to call *me*; it was a 307 area code and so I picked up. I was still fragile after Kiley's death, and would be for a while, and Dad knew that, so I believe he found a way to call me without making excuses of why he didn't or couldn't be there for me.

It was the beginning of the week when he called and the second time we had spoken in a week. He was happy, but I still sensed an anxiousness and urgency: "Have you sent it yet?"

Dad was very proud that his daughter was the author of a *published* story in a *Chicken Soup for the Soul* book. There was a reason, however, that I delayed in sending it. The story was about a cat, but the characters were me, Mom and Danny, my stepdad. Mom and Danny had been married six years. I was in my late 20s when they got married and I wasn't sure if that made him my "stepdad" or not; I was too old to accept, want or need another father figure. Still, over the years, it felt right and genuine to refer to Danny as my stepdad and not just "mom's husband". With his eyeglasses and sneakers, Danny didn't have any similarities to the Cowboy—he didn't drink for one. He was born and raised Wyoming, but had no sign of cowboy charisma. Danny was not only reliable, he was *content*. My dad was a free-spirited wanderer who didn't want to be roped and tied down, just like the calf he caught in the rodeo. He wanted to roam free as the cattle on the open range.

More than ever, the Cowboy struggled through his grief, sadness, and awareness; he was surprisingly also allowing for sober emotions to show themselves and resisted fighting them with the bottle. These were all actually bittersweet hints of healing, but I didn't want to offer a story, which did not include him, and could consequently taint his slow progress. I knew this Cowboy so well and I sensed, monitored, and heard any movement he made over the phone. My child-of-an-alcoholic radar warned me to be cautious—it had just become second-nature.

Our conversations in the past year though, had become truthful, compassionate, sweet and lovely. I was in a place where I could trust that and share my thoughts with him. So I told him that the reason I hadn't sent it was that I was afraid it would hurt his feelings.

I explained, "Mom and her husband are part of the story."

"I don't care about that, Hun. Please just send it," he said softly.

So I confirmed the "Rowdy Broughton General Delivery Laramie Wyoming" address.

I was busy at work, and didn't have a chance until Saturday. That morning I sat in a quiet space, to write a note in the book to my Dad the Cowboy, reminding him again, that *he* was also a part of *my* story. On page 261 of *Chicken Soup for the Soul: What I learned from the Cat*, is my cat story titled, "Homeward Bound" and on the blank page beside that, I dated "November 14, 2009" and wrote:

Dear Dad,

I hope you enjoy the message conveyed in my story. More importantly though I hope you know that I got my creativity from you. When I write I think of you. When I read this story, it reminds me also of growing up with cats and Blue – the first Persian cat you got me by trading a pair of chaps for! I love you Dad and I miss you!

Melissa

I slid the book into a padded envelope, giggled when I wrote "Rowdy" Broughton, I imagined him opening it, reading my message and loving it—oh I just couldn't wait for him to get it!

That afternoon, on the way to the post office, my phone rang.

"Helloo," I answered in a happy-go-lucky tone.

It was my Aunt Kathleen, whom I knew well, but rarely spoke to—the last time I spoke with her I may have been in my mid 20s.

"Hi Sweetie … your dad had a seizure on Thursday and he's in the hospital in Laramie," Aunt Kathleen said without pause, explaining that the hospital had just gotten in touch with her that day.

Aunt Kathleen's message was short, and I couldn't gauge her emotions in her voice—I was usually very good at knowing or feeling where people were coming from.

Panic and shock overtook me, and for the first time in my life, I could not react to a crisis; I couldn't focus or decide what to do or how to do it. Seconds seemed like hours and as the moments passed I was frustrated by my paralysis. My co-dependent problem-solving skills were stunned and left me abandoned. It doesn't happen very often, but sometimes a cow will give birth and then just leave the calf lying there, wet, cold and hungry, shaking in the field. In that moment, what I had depended on much of my life—my ability to buck up—had left me.

I imagined the Cowboy, in a hospital, and it snapped me out of my trance; I needed to get to him as soon as possible.

I didn't make it to the post office to mail the book to the Cowboy that afternoon. Instead I rushed to Laramie, Wyoming where I hoped to deliver it in person. I stuffed a few things in a small bag, including the book that I would now personally deliver to the Cowboy that I hadn't seen in five years, but to the Dad I had spoken to just days before.

Miraculously I found a flight that day—to Denver where I met R.J. and Mom and Danny. I had contacted R.J. and Mom shortly after I got *the call*; I don't remember what was said, but it relayed what was necessary—this is it. The Cowboy. We need to get to Laramie ASAP.

We fled from Colorado to Wyoming through the blinding of the snow, skidding on patches of black ice. I stared out the back window of the truck, zoning out from the bright, white drifts of snow. Everyone remained in a silent daze, wondering what we would discover. I pictured him, the Dad I had not seen in five years: brown hair with a hat ring, blonde mustache, and tan skin with his character wrinkles.

I sat in the back seat of the extended cab truck, glaring at the hills covered in white, glistening snow and every now and then I would snap out of my hypnosis and think, "Is this really happening?" There were SUVs slid into the side of the road who clearly thought their big tires would get them through black ice. I felt as if the Cowboy were calling out: "Hurry. Hurry!"

We arrived at the Laramie hospital, parked and ran in with a strange hesitation. I knew how I *felt*—scared, overwhelmed, shocked, sad and in denial—but I didn't know how to act or behave. I didn't know what to expect and I felt like my actions were being watched—"Watch to see what Melissa does and says, she always knows what to do." I was afraid I would lose control in some way, and all of these complex feelings made me feel like a zombie, lost and roaming the hospital halls.

And there he was—my Dad the Cowboy, lying in the bed, unconscious. I hesitated to run to him for a second, but then I just threw myself and my arms around him as much as I could, snuggled my head on his chest and wept.

"I'm sorry, I'm sorry I didn't get here sooner," I sobbed—I don't know if I said that out loud or just to myself.

My tears soaked his chest as I lay there, not wanting to move. I actually thought that if I tried hard enough, that maybe he would sense the emotion radiating from me and wake up.

"Please, please wake up," I kept repeating. And then I turned my plea to God and begged the same prayer, over and over. I didn't want to take my eyes off of him; I sat and stared, admiring every single thing that I had missed those five years. He was older and tired.

The Cowboy did not look like I remembered him, or how I envisioned Dad when we spoke on the phone. Now, his hair was no longer brown, but inconceivably *beautiful*; it was slightly longer than a grown-out clean-cut and it was fairly white, with a very light hue of cream color and a few silver strands here and there that I might have missed had I not been within inches of his face. This was not an "old person's" grey and white. It was creamy with silver, thick and wavy, long enough to run your fingers through. It looked almost angelic, just like his mom's hair; my grandma had signature creamy white hair –thick, striking color.

His mustache was still blonde, but wirey and sporadic—a few hairs were singed—and his face was slightly red and bloated from capillaries expanding. He had very few wrinkles, only his wonderful smile lines.

The blankets covered up to mid-chest and his bare skin was white, just as usual, but I could see that his shoulder was uneven and crooked; I knew he had been bucked off a horse a few years prior and broke his shoulder as he complained about this pain when we spoke on the phone. Mom and R.J. took everything in, too, and hardly spoke.

"Randy …Hun …we're here," Mom whispered, tears in her eyes as she smoothed her hand over his several times and then held it.

My eyes followed down his arms where his white skin faded into a farmer tan down through his hands and fingers. And his hands revealed the same hands I had known as a child—rancher hands of a hard-working cowboy. Tan, strong and curved inward on their way to making a fist. R.J. cried, gasping for air as he hesitantly touched the Cowboy's shoulder, then forehead, as if the skin to skin contact would cause an emotional eruption.

The doc was called in on his day off; he was wearing Wrangler jeans, boots and a western shirt; had he been wearing his lab coat though, the mustache still would have given it away—that we were actually in Wyoming.

"You do realize that he has been in the ER several times for these seizures brought on by withdrawal from alcohol?" The handle-bar mustached doctor explained with little tolerance.

Mom, R.J. and I were still within a few feet from Dad when we sat down to talk with the doc. It was confusing to have the Cowboy so close while we discussed the consequences of his alcoholism.

Dr. Handle-bar Mustache's annoyance was obvious and I understood that completely. "Your dad is a very, very sick man; I probably don't have to tell you that he is an alcoholic," he said sternly to make sure we understood.

I responded with an intense stare back and a strong nod of my head to convey, that not only did I completely understand, but that I would do *anything* to make it right and make the Cowboy well.

"I have told your dad every time he comes in here what he is doing to his body and what he *needs* to do. Quite frankly I'm getting tired of this," Dr. Intense-Mustache continued.

Dr. You've-caught-my-patience-on-a-bad-day-and-I'm-tired-of-taking-care-of-people-who-clearly-don't-want-to-take-care-of-themselves, summarized his thoughts with, "and right now we are dealing with respiratory distress and shock; Randy, your dad, drinks heavily and then tries to quit cold turkey. And if we can *actually* pull him through this time, I *guarantee* there will not be a next time. *Do you understand?*"

The whole time the doc was talking I was listening intently to his instruction, but also wanted to really *show* him—that the Cowboy would pull through this like he had many other situations.

The doc softened his tone a little, "Your dad is basically suffering from the effects of alcoholism, but right now what's killing him are the withdrawals; a person can actually die from the withdrawals of two drugs—heroin and alcohol."

I looked over at the Cowboy and shook my head, completely overwhelmed.

Finally, Dr. Mustache sighed and said what I'm sure most docs do when they are concluding their information lecture: "But ... we will do everything we can for your dad."

The seizures actually started in 2005; it was what seemed to be another rock bottom event that triggered the sincere desire to want and get help. The lure and disease though, from my perspective, is more vindictive, stronger than dozens of rock bottom ah-has. I had forgotten the Cowboy told me in a letter that he had had a seizure—one sent just months after he left me at the Greyhound Bus station.

May 29, 2005
Melissa & RJ
    Well I finally got the courage to write you. Both of you kids will get this letter. I admitted myself into rehab about two weeks ago. During my detox I had a seizure. I don't have to tell you it scared me to death. I was lucky enough to get into a program called TRT. I have to be here for another 4 weeks. After that, I will be transferred to a sobriety house. For 6 weeks, 3 hours a night, 4 nights a week I will be in therapy and education alcohol classes. At that time I will also be able to look for work. It has been real hard for me but I know that I have to do it. I have met some good people here. Men and women, and the counselors are great. I hope everything is good with both of you. I love you. Dad

I could not bring myself to believe the longevity of the potential results proposed in this letter. I could not fully appreciate the gift of the present thinking and planning the Cowboy had at the moment he wrote the hopeful words on the paper. I was still confused by anger, disappointment and hurt from *my* rock bottom experience with the Cowboy when I shipped him away on the Greyhound bus after his disease denied my help and puked on my carpet.

    The shelf life of Dad's rock bottom mentality—"Boy did that show me; I'll never do that again!"—got shorter and shorter with each incident. My wavering hope was the same, but fortunately, no matter how deep it dove to rock bottom, it always surfaced again.

    One nurse, clearly smitten with the unconscious cowboy, mentioned his hair and mustache all the while pleading with me to get some sleep. With a bobbing head, I fought sleep on the couch in the visitor's waiting room just feet away from Dad. It was the first night with the Cowboy and everyone was sure he would awaken and I surely didn't want to miss that—his surprised face when he saw me, R.J. and our mom in the hospital room. I fantasized that this scene would be the final rock bottom and it would give him inspiration to be awake in his own life.

I listened to the background hospital noises, which seemed to have the effect of a lullaby, and I drifted off.

What felt like seconds later, the nurse startled me; she tried to be gentle in putting her hand on my shoulder, saying, "Honey, it's your Dad."

At that moment it was as if someone put a defibrillator on my heart and I woke up instantly.

"Sweetie … your dad couldn't breathe on his own and the doc did what he was hoping he would not have to do—he put him on a ventilator."

When I saw the Cowboy with breathing tubes, I threw myself on him again and begged God for mercy. Somehow, I fainted—the nurses swooped to my side. I revived within seconds, and laid my head on the Cowboy's chest.

"Honey, now, now, take a deeeep breath," the nurse comforted, feeling my forehead and then smoothing back my hair.

"Honey you have got to get some rest," she offered.

"Please, let me stay here with my dad; I will sleep I promise, just please let me stay."

I sat in a chair next to Dad's bed and hunched my arms and head over onto his chest and fell asleep.

My dreams of waking up to the Cowboy alert and delighted by my being there were crushed when I opened my eyes and he was still lying there, motionless and expressionless. I vowed to not leave or fall asleep again as I had just before he stopped breathing.

I needed a shower, but didn't want to leave, so the nurses offered the facilities just across the hall, just feet away from the Cowboy. I took a two-minute shower and washed my hair with bar soap only to come back to see that Dad now needed dialysis.

A ventilator and dialysis! I really didn't understand the seriousness of these scary-looking machines next to Dad's bed and naively continued to hope.

Another drunken cowboy showed up in the ICU for a visit; Dave was one of Dad's best buds. He slurred his words sharing with Mom that "Rowdy always talked about you being the love of his life."

It was something Mom already knew, but it was strangely endearing to hear it, even from the Cowboy's alcoholic buddy. Dave stayed awhile and his presence was, in an ironic way, not disruptive at all despite his blubbering. He allowed me to drift from reality and imagine him and Dad laughing and joking over a few beers. His few words were comforting—he was the last one to talk with the Cowboy.

Dave noticed as I massaged Dad's hands. "Oh he said that his little girl always massaged his feet and hands. Ten-ten, right?"

And a few minutes later he hiccupped, "Did you really live in Italy?"

As strange as it seemed at the time, hearing that from Dad's drunken cowboy friend meant Dad had shared stories with him about me. I continued massaging the Cowboy's white feet.

The doctors were all general practitioners and at this point I didn't even realize the importance of "specialists." The docs did explain that he was having multiple organ failure due to the withdrawal symptoms, but they were still hopeful and the ventilator and dialysis were seen as temporary. Hearing the word "temporary" was important for me; I knew Dad never wanted to be on life support.

By the third day, the docs lost hope too fast and were not offering options for the Cowboy's need for extended dialysis care now.

"If this hospital doesn't have the resources for this care, then where is the closest hospital that does?" I asked, annoyed that I was the one asking these questions instead of them offering me the options.

One doctor offered, "Well, Fort Collins is the best we can do."

Depending on the weather, Fort Collins, Colorado is a couple of hours from Laramie.

I hadn't a clue where the hospitals were or what they offered. It was that little voice, that gut feeling that told me there was a better option—why wasn't it being presented?

By this point I was stubborn and taking charge more than I ever had before. Even though this may be just another drunk who is homeless and irresponsible, the Cowboy was my father. Divinely at that moment, another nurse, whom I noticed the day before, thought out loud while she wrote notes on patients (one observes a lot when you sit in a hospital room 24/7), whispered while she took Dad's vitals, "Why don't they send him to Cheyenne?"

I heard that! I thought *quietly*. So, I insisted on a transfer to the hospital in Cheyenne, Wyoming, which offered a staff of specialists and was not as far as Fort Collins; they did not argue and I wondered why they didn't offer the option in the first place.

Next thing I knew, Dick the Deacon, who always started his sentences with "It's a long story…" offered a Buddhist prayer. And then we followed an ambulance for a two- hour drive to Cheyenne Regional Medical Center to meet and live in the Progressive Care Unit for almost two weeks.

Nineteen

The journey to Cheyenne, all these years later, reminded me of the time we left the desert for familiar territory—Cowboy territory—when I was a child. I remembered when we left the desert all those years ago. Headed back to Colorado to a small, non-working ranch outside of Pueblo, Colorado, we were still driving that god-for-saken old car with a thunderbird painted on it, and the dirt road off the highway seemed like it would never end. When we first moved there, I felt relieved to be back in Colorado, back in the countryside. The house was small, two bedrooms, one bathroom and a tiny kitchen. We got there around the holidays and I remember our small Christmas tree. My parents were money-less—it had been the "less than a year" from hell, from the ranch to the armpit of the world, with a car repossessed and little work for months. I made homemade ornaments for the desperate tree. We didn't care though; I think my family was so happy and relieved to be back to something familiar—dirt road, smell of a ranch, cats and a cattle dog running around. My parents were happy again; they were affectionate and no longer arguing. It was six months of healing from the shock of "life outside of the country" we had all experienced in Arizona. It was like we were in rehab at a secluded ranch, detoxing from culture desert shock.

———◆———

I remember sitting on the saw buck fence that stood a few yards between the ranch house and the field; Dad built saw buck fences which outlined most parts of the ranch. Many summer hours were spent stripping pine trees into poles and constructing them together, like a puzzle piece, with no nails. Each fence was a unique, hand-made piece of art. Each pine pole was criss-crossed with another, creating beautiful lines in distant pastures. The Flying W was the only ranch in the Valley lucky enough to have an old-fashioned cowboy contribute the time and effort to make the saw buck fences; most went with all barbed-wire. The saw buck fence was one of my favorite places to play around or just "be".

Dad drove by in the old ranch truck, squinting, with his hat on, the window rolled down. He stopped the truck at the saw buck. He didn't need to ask, he knew. Just the fact that I was hanging out on the saw buck was a sign for him to check in. "Hey there young lady," he said.

"Dad, I need a good idea for the science fair project. I have to come up with a hypothesis."

"Ya know Honey, those been extinct fer years," he said, making himself laugh, adding, "Dontcha worry Honey we'll come up with somethin'. Be in for supper in a bit." And that was all the reassurance I needed.

After supper that night, Dad and I went outside and looked at the stars, "What's your favorite star?"

Not really knowing a lot about astronomy, I picked the obvious—The Big Dipper and Little Dipper.

A month later I placed fifth in the local Science Fair with the hypothesis on how much those two bodies of stars moved throughout the night. Dad and I measured them with a home-made sextant that the Cowboy taught me to make with a protractor, straw, fishing line and a weight. Every night for a month, Dad and I would go outside after supper at 7:00, 8:00 and 9:00, look through the straw taped on top of the protractor as if it were a telescope and the weight at the end of the fishing line would hang at a different angle every hour. It was a project Dad did when he was in elementary, a simple concept really, but to a fifth grader, it was as brilliant as the night sky.

Twenty

I had never felt closer to the Cowboy's true self. Seeing him again—in the flesh—his rugged cowboy face, blonde mustache and wavy, white hair and hard-working hands; I was witnessing his silent detox.

The grief I was experiencing was so intense that I could feel it physically punching my insides—each punch carrying with it the force of fear and sadness.

When Dad had shared information about his seizures during our phone calls, I was always trying to gage the seriousness; I hadn't a clue what could be causing continued seizures. Dad explained that he visited the community clinic and they would give him anti-seizure medication and send him on his way. My head and heart battled whether I should visit or not: should I leave work, how can I afford it, will my presence help him or make it worse, where will I stay if I go, what will I do to help?

As I lay next to the Cowboy, I thought about Kiley's life and death. I think some people know that they are about to leave this earth. I mean, not consciously, but there is something about their aura, energy, reveals the little secret that they will be gone soon.

When I was with Kiley through a chemo treatment and everything *seemed* to be looking up and improving, I laid my head on her lap and she trickled her fingers through my hair, comforting me through pain that was to come weeks later. A sliver of her spirit slid through her fingers, glided from the roots through the strands of fine, blonde and to the ends of my hair; I felt the rise of goose bumps and a subconscious hint of peace and for just a second, I heard the words: "Kiley's suffering will stop."

But then the information faded and I just lay there as my best friend twisted and twirled my hair. The same kind of whispering messages were slowly being passed to me every day from the Cowboy.

———◆———

The Cowboy was *supposed* to die on November 20th. The Cheyenne Hospital did not allow me to stay the night and so I stayed at a nearby hotel with R.J., Mom and Danny, my stepdad; it was only a seven-minute drive to the hospital, but it still felt too far.

My cell phone rang at 4:00am. "It's your Dad; he's had a seizure and heart attack and we resuscitated."

It woke me from a half-sleep slumber and back into my crisis mode; this attack was not expected and so there were no "directions" from me to resuscitate or not, and so they did. "We are sure it will happen again, and we think this is it; you should come to the hospital right away."

I didn't need to get dressed; I slept in my clothes and shoes, ready.

The call came again. "He's having a heart attack again, what do you want us to do?" they asked in a calm but urgent, well-practiced manner.

I had not signed anything or had a conversation with a doctor or my family about what to do. "Resuscitate! We are on our way!"

I had learned in Laramie that I would be the decision maker for life and death choices for the Cowboy; he was divorced and I was his oldest child. As hard as these decisions were, this honor created a war between my head and heart. I wanted him to live; I needed him to wake up and see that I came to him.

Icy side street roads or not, I was insisting Danny drive faster. I actually considered jumping out of the truck while it was still moving, I visualized myself running, felt the cold in my lungs as I breathed in—"faster, faster, I have to run faster" I heard myself saying.

By the time we arrived, mere minutes after the Cowboy had the heart attack, he was stable.

This was one of the few times that I hadn't slept over in the hospital; I leaned over and whispered in Dad's ear, "I promise I'm not going anywhere; I'm right here."

"What's the date?" I asked when the nurse walked in, "November 20th." Without hesitation, Mom said: "That's grandma's birthday."

The Cowboy had been extremely close with his mom; when she passed away a few years prior, the Cowboy's alcoholism found yet another excuse to rage. His grief for his mom became another weapon against himself. I insisted they resuscitate—I still had emotional *and* medical hope that the Cowboy had a chance, but still, I wondered if the Cowboy was meant to go on the day of his mother's birthday. I remembered one day in Grandma's bedroom; I was ten years old or so. "An angel visited me," she'd said, sitting next to me at the end of her bed. "I was having a real hard time with your grandpa, and an angel, surrounded by light—I could hardly see it was so bright—came to me, picked me up, and held me." Her glazed look told me that she was putting herself back in that moment as she spoke. "I knew then that no matter what happened, I would be okay." The hairs on my little neck had stood up and I knew this was no made-up grandma story.

Still trying to negotiate with God, my sincere, relentless hope turned to desperation; now it wasn't a matter of the Cowboy waking up, now I was just begging God that the Cowboy would wake up to see that his children came to be with him, so that I could just tell him I love him.

I could see my brother's and my Mom's pain as well. With his pronounced nose and blue eyes, R.J. looked like the Cowboy. "Well, you're a spittin image of your dad ain't ya?" one of the nursing aids said. He never wanted to be a cowboy or look like a cowboy when he was little or a teenager. He rebelled against the rodeo and ranch lifestyle, but in his 20s, he started wearing boots, a vest and a cowboy hat. And now, a grown up, he sounded just like the Cowboy. Like the cows and horses that meandered in the pasture, R.J. roamed in his boots around the Cowboy's bed, concentrating on him and perhaps wondering just how much he really was like his Dad.

Mom paced, cried, shook her head. Still petite, more now frail and her brunette waves faded into a small bun, Mom sat next to Dad's bed, holding his hand, rubbing his forehead. She concentrated on him as if communicating telepathically. R.J. and I left the room; we listened, the Cowboy's hospital door ajar. There was nothing to hear. Nothing to decipher.

And *nothing* changed; *nothing* happened.

The Cowboy still laid there, vitals the same—dialysis, heart monitor, respiratory machines all just beeping in unison, communicating life and death.

I had come to understand well, the machines keeping the Cowboy alive—so much that even one of the doctors thought I knew more than I actually did.

"Clearly you are in the medical field," Dad's doc said when I rattled off his varying vitals and schedules for everything from heart, lung and dialysis. If I looked at those machines today, I wouldn't have a clue as to what I was reading.

"Had he been coughing?" one of the docs asked and I remembered Dad coughing and laughing during our phone conversations.

"Yes, for a few months now."

The doctors offered a possible answer to only a portion of the Cowboy's ailments; "Your Dad has Acute Respiratory Distress Syndrome ... or what we call ARDS, and it's making it quite difficult for him to breathe on his own."

"What causes that?" I assumed it was cigarette smoking.

"Actually, living in cold conditions and developing pneumonia—we see it a lot with the homeless population here in Cheyenne." I wondered if maybe Dad had been sick—had undiagnosed pneumonia or something—at the time he was trying to detox.

Then the doctor inquired about the alcohol consumption, withdrawals and seizures; "What can you tell me about that?" he'd ask, working from a blank, untainted slate, unlike Dr. Handlebar Mustache. He wanted to know what was going on from my perspective, not the hospital in Laramie. Here, the Cowboy had a team—a pulmonologist, a nephrologist for dialysis, a surgeon, two respiratory therapists, and three male nurses.

And the doc ended his questions with, "We're glad you're here; they simply do not have the resources needed to care for your father in Laramie."

At that moment, I had confirmation that I made the right impulsive decision to transfer the "really nothing is going to help" Laramie Cowboy to Cheyenne.

I strategically taped photos of me, R.J. and Dad's handsome cowboy photo at the end of Dad's bed so that it would be the first thing he saw when he did wake up because after all, surely God would grant at least that. The black and white photo of Dad in his cowboy hat with the snakeskin hatband was taped at the end of his bed, in the middle as if it were a target I'd hoped his eyes would find as soon as he opened them, a reminder of the great cowboy he was. Another photo taped to the left of that of R.J. and I being chum-chum, to remind him of the happy kids he created. And on the right side, a picture of me in cowboy boots fishing on the Rio Grande River to remind him of the country life that he loved.

I rubbed the Cowboy's feet and hands, whispering "ten-ten" and hoping he felt it.

The nurses always talked to him like he was awake, "Okay Cowboy, we're gonna give ya a shot and you might feel a little pinch."

I was hoping he would open his eyes and yell "Ouch! What the hell was that for?" But he just lay there.

Besides being with the Cowboy, the highlight of my day was the nursing aides coming in to wash the Cowboy's hair and shave his face, leaving his mustache. The rule was that R.J. and I had to leave the room while this was done, but the before and after giddiness of the aides made me smile because I knew how much the Cowboy would get a kick out of it.

I remembered when I was a kid, how he'd lean over the sink, into the mirror, his cheeks and chin covered with shaving cream. I'd linger in the doorway, watching the Cowboy shave section by section, leaving his mustache. The sink was full of water and floating, dollops of shaving cream; he did a quick rinse of his razor in the water and then shaved the other cheek as if it were a pasture, row by row cutting the field of alfalfa.

"Damn, I'm-a good lookin' son of a bitch," he'd say and chuckle, pausing to look to his reflection, and then shifting his eyes at me.

"Daaaad!" I loved when he teased saying that.

In junior high, I would walk by the bathroom during his shaving ritual and he'd say the same thing; I'd roll my eyes, and laugh saying, "You're such a dork."

"What, it's true, ain't it Honey?" he'd quip, walking into the kitchen and kissing Mom on her cheek, leaving her with shaving cream on her face.

"If you say so," she'd tease, knowing that she didn't need to reassure him of his dashing looks.

"Do you know your dad looks just like Sam Elliott?" the nurse's aide asked after his wash and shave.

I laughed just a little; "Ya, we've heard that a time or two."

The aides changed on different shifts and they all said the same thing. "This is our job and we love it, but we *love* washing your Dad's beautiful hair."

"Boy, would he love to hear you say that," I said.

———————◆———————

My brother and I lived in the hospital—beeping sounds of monitors in the background, the smell of everything being sanitized from germs and emotions and divider curtains between each "will they or won't they live" patients. For two weeks we stayed in critical care; there were a couple of nights in the beginning when we abided by patient visiting hours, but it seemed that every time we left, the Cowboy's will to live dwindled. Eventually, we stayed there all day and all night, maximizing every moment with the Cowboy and only leaving for a few minutes when tests had to be done.

R.J. and I even attempted normalcy on Thanksgiving Day, going to the hospital cafeteria to eat turkey dinner. I don't even think the food was bad, but we were back in Dad's room within fifteen minutes; we celebrated Thanksgiving with Dad by remembering our Thanksgiving dinners as a family growing up—it was always just the four of us, staying at the ranch, never travelling and eating a delicious turkey and ham dinner.

The doctors and nurses allowed us to bond with them temporarily; we saw them all day every day and they too, wanted the Cowboy to wake up so they could meet him. My brother and I were regular fixtures in the room, and other patients' families would come to visit their loved ones who were recovering and even looked at us like, "You're still here? Have you even left for a break?"

I still prayed and begged; mainly because I was delirious and it was the only thing I had left, not because I believed it would work. As time went on, it was clear that God was not going to answer my crying plea. I started to lose my faith. I did not blame God for the pain, addiction or consequences nor did I think this was punishment for the Cowboy's sins or my sins; I was not that naïve or spiritually immature. I did, however, feel *entitled* to grace.

"Your dad is the sickest man in Cheyenne," Dr. Tetenta said with a bit of a not-quite-yet-defeated sigh.

Dr. Tetenta, originally from Nigeria, was the brilliant, calming pulmonologist working with the Cowboy's lungs for over a week. So serious, with a sincere friendly smile if you could catch it, Dr. Tetenta seemed to be a man of faith, knew how to say things in a way that transcended the literal. "Even though he has had one heart attack, his heart really is the strongest and most amazing organ that he has left. But it is supporting the others and getting tired."

Dad's heart trying to rescue the other organs! It *was* the Cowboy's heart and charisma that made everyone love him, but mostly my mother, and my brother and I. It was his heartbreak that prompted more drinking and consequently seizures and I was reminded what he said: "Every time I think about what I've lost, I have a seizure."

The Cowboy's body was detoxing and he looked like a healthy, young fifty-four- year-old cowboy laying there in his bed. The Cowboy's organs were failing; he was dying, but his body had time to rest for almost two weeks without alcohol. Into the second week, "The sickest man in Cheyenne" looked handsome and the "normal" Cowboy that we knew—beautiful milky skin, no bloating, and his, now well-known, wavy white hair and blonde mustache.

I was reaching emotional and physical exhaustion and I could see my brother was too. I stopped praying and started pacing; I didn't pack anything from California—I had the same clothes on for two weeks and I needed to check in at work.

R.J. and I came up with a plan to go back home, pack a few necessities, tie up loose ends temporarily, and then return to Cheyenne within a day or two.

I shared this idea with Dr. Tetenta, "I can understand why you need to do this; you have been here for two weeks, but I just want to let you know that our loved ones often wait for us to leave and then they pass away."

Dr. Tetenta hugged each of us and R.J. sobbed, "Thank you for everything you have done for my dad." We were so torn; it was a simple, but risky plan.

R.J. and I spent that morning with our Dad the Cowboy; we talked with him together and cried and then separately we loved on him as much as possible and kissed him good-bye, "I love you and we'll be back soon."

As I walked away, I heard the same whisper I heard the day Kiley was twirling my hair, "Your dad's suffering will end"; it was such a faint whisper that it came and went and I forged ahead with my mission to get home and then get back to the Cowboy.

We reluctantly drove out of Wyoming, heading for Denver. It was a Saturday.

The only thing I remember after that is sitting on my bedroom floor in Santa Barbara with my suitcase, thinking about how to take a leave of absence from my life in California; I was in a denial fog, but still methodical, determined.

I was spent in every way, but didn't feel it. What I did feel was strange being in my apartment; it was uncomfortable and awkward and I missed being in Dad's room and watching over him, with the nurses close by—I was uneasy and antsy, which left me paralyzed in making decisions. Sunday came and before my bag was packed and my flight was booked, my phone rang—a 307 area code.

"Your dad has had a heart attack and we resuscitated him. We suspect it will happen again soon, so you should come in right away," a doctor explained.

After two weeks of care with the Cowboy, the staff had rotated and there were different nurses and a different pulmonologist with Dad.

"I left yesterday. I am in California. I can't get back right *now*."

For a split second I imagined I could get on a plane in the next half hour and be there in two hours.

"I need to know what you want us to do when it happens again."

I suppose they sensed my complete inability to know what to do, and so the female doctor offered, "Honey, it is time for your

Dad to go; he is tired and so is his heart. We can resuscitate again, but it will just happen again."

When I heard those words I knew she was right, but I still hated her in that moment; I sat on my floor and sobbed. My heart felt cold, cracked like the frozen pond I once skated on.

Then, in the background, I could hear the emergency beeping of the heart monitor, "It's happening again! Honey, what do you want us to do?"

I spoke carefully through my tears, "Ok, ok, you can stop, yes you can stop resuscitation."

"We will call you right back..." she said fading off the phone. I just lay there sobbing; I could not cry hard enough to match the pain.

My Dad the Cowboy, the sickest man in Cheyenne, died of alcoholism that afternoon, November 29th.

Twenty-One

I sat on the floor of my small apartment, contemplating opening a box of my Cowboy's only belongings, which had been mailed to me a week after his death. I wanted to just wrap my arms around that tattered cardboard box—bandaged with silver duct tape. Whatever the contents were, they were Dad's. So I did; I grasped the box, stretching my arms around its corners, as the box and I sat on the floor. I rested my head on top of the box, and cried hard for a while.

Slowly, I unraveled the box—tearing the strips of tape off, piece by piece, and then opening each flap, one by one. I longed for connection with Dad, and knew his energy was once with these things—these papers and such which meant nothing to anyone else, but also hinted at his demise. I stared a little more, lifting my hand hesitantly as if it had a ten-pound weight pulling it down, to open the next flap. The cardboard box now completely open, and my head just collapsed on the corner of it, hugging it again.

I can take all the time I need, I thought.

Old cigarette smoke drifted away from the box, barely graced the air along with the smell of four unwashed flannel shirts and a jean jacket—as if he had just had them on. I searched each pocket, feeling around, stretching the fabric, hoping to find anything of the Cowboy's. Tobacco pieces, probably from a cigarette he kept in his pocket, and his handkerchief. The Cowboy always carried a handkerchief; I clutched the soft, off-white cloth in my hand, closed my eyes and breathed it in.

And then I remembered, his flannel shirts, the ones I had packed for him in the duffle bag that he clutched in the Santa Barbara five years before. I remembered his desperate jean jacket, and his handkerchief that had peaked out of the jean jacket pocket that day in the bus station.

A collection of papers revealed only the sad circumstances the Cowboy had lived during his last years: ranch job applications; a reminder note to himself for AA meetings at 7:30 p.m.at Trinity Lutheran; payment schedule for a DUI fine; disability papers from being bucked off a horse; approval letter for food stamps; hospital bills; and a letter I had mailed him a few years earlier.

Each piece of paper from the box told a story or explained something. I made myself read them; I wanted to know, to feel—if possible—what he had gone through. My face was soaked and blubberings came out of my nose and mouth. I read desperation in the job applications; Dad answered "Anything" in the blank line for "Positions applied for" and for "Work Performed" he listed all of the things a cattleman does—all the things he did for years, including being a member of the Professional Rodeo Cowboys Association since 1976.

And in a cover letter written on unlined typing paper, the Cowboy wrote with a shaky hand, "There has been no ranch work, but I never give up. I had a stroke, but still have my brain; I just can't walk too good. The best thing I have is my heart and my experience."

I held these papers to my chest, trying to feel and imagine when he wrote these words and touched these papers. And the note from me that he kept, also written on typing paper:

Hi Dad! Here are a few things for you! The vitamin K cream is for your face or where you have psoriasis and the milk thistle is for your liver.
Love,
Melissa

I remembered sending that note to him and how, at that moment, I hoped like hell that he felt my concern for him. And the hospital bills, many of them unopened, revealed several visits to the ER the past two years for drunken falls, sudden seizures and alcohol withdrawals and even notes "Randy reports that..." from a therapist from a community center he sought help from for his addiction.

———◆———

I wondered about my grief and how it fit around my beliefs of heaven and the afterlife of Kiley and Dad. My sadness around Kiley was expected, normal grief; it was a deep sadness for the loss of my best friend. I missed Kiley and my grief was tears of missing our friendship and for the loss felt by her husband, children, mom, sister and all who loved her. Disbelief and then realization that she was gone; my sadness was intense, but strangely in-check. My sadness with the loss of my father took on a different disguise. I could not comprehend the pain, which left me feeling alone and debilitated.

Four flannel shirts, a handkerchief, a jean jacket, pictures, notes and a mound of paperwork—those were Dad's belongings in the end.

———◆———

I t was February—almost three months after the Cowboy's death, and I'd organized a service at the Cowboy Church on the Flying W Ranch in Colorado Springs, the same place where Dad started his cowboy career making biscuits for visitors at the Ranch.

Now, we weren't going with desperate hope in our hearts; we were traveling aimlessly to the acknowledgement of his death. This quote comes from the movie *The Cowboys*. R.J. picked this quote to share at the memorial service—it was our Dad's favorite movie:

> *Sometimes it's hard to understand the drift of things. Death can come for ya any place, any time. It's never welcomed. But if you've done all you can do, and it's your best, in a way I guess you're ready for it. --Wil Andersen (John Wayne)*

We arrived to the Cowboy Church. I conveyed a slight, forced smile for attendees of the memorial service, all the while searching for an escape of the empathetic eye contact. Heartache crept in like random knife jabs to my side.

I remembered the regret I felt taking the Cowboy to a barbershop on Milpas Street; I was embarrassed that his hair was greasy and long. It was during the short time the Cowboy lived with me in Santa Barbara; he was looking pretty rough and needed a shampoo, cut and a shave. I lived just off Mission street in Santa Barbara—it was pretty much the middle of town, but instead of taking Dad conveniently to a barbershop near where I lived and worked, I went out of my way to go to a barbershop on Milpas Street; for some, Milpas can "seem" the not-so-good part of town (putting things into perspective, no such "part" really exists in Santa Barbara).

There was a slight awareness of my wanting to keep my alcoholic, homeless and seedy-looking father away from anyone who knew me. We walked into an old barbershop where an old Mexican man offered service—no appointment needed.

As if his "homelessness" made him unable to speak for himself, I did the talking; with English a bit of a challenge for the barber I explained slowly what the Cowboy needed. And so I paid $14 for a shampoo, cut and shave, with just a trim off the mustache.

During the memorial service, and long after, I kept circling around the idea that Dad, ultimately, was defeated by withdrawals of alcoholism, which left me confused by the idea of how I should "feel" about the *way* he died. Dying from withdrawals meant he was trying to quit drinking and I knew that from our phone conversations. It was like losing by one point. Dad, being a cowboy, tried to quit cold turkey—too fast, too soon, and without supervised detox and rehab. There were hopeful things in his life—our phone calls, a new will to live—but his physical body and dependence rejected such a grand plan.

My *dad* was gone; the man I chased my whole life, trying to catch up to him, wrangle him and trying to keep him—I felt as though I had never caught him and now he was gone for infinity. My heart felt stomped on—I could visualize it—Alcoholism, punched its fist through my chest cavity, stopped my heart's beating with its grip and ripped it from my body. Alcoholism crushed it with its bare claws. The ache of the anxiety and agony loomed in my chest and it was too much to bear alone. I paced with my options in my mind as to what I could do to end this unfamiliar and overwhelming misery. I realized I would need support to get through this spirit-suffocating *thing*. I needed help: to start taking care of *me*.

Twenty-Two

Tell me something I don't already know. I would never say this out loud, but certainly thought as the years went by when a friend or therapist offered that my issues with men and self-esteem contributed to my young marriage, divorce, running away and out-of-character behavior and stemmed from "daughter of an alcoholic father" issues.

After Dad left Santa Barbara, I tried a support group for "adult children of alcoholics". It felt strange and uncomfortable. I sat in the circle of folding chairs in a Unity church, my shoulders tensed up to my ears, my fingers gripped the edge of the chair and I listened and never offered a peep. *Just try it. Stay with it. Have an open mind*, I thought. That was followed by: *This is so fucking uncomfortable, not helping me at all, and I'm annoyed that I can't leave because I am sitting in a fucking circle."*

The circle group didn't help and *California* self-reflection and therapy helped only a smidgen for me in my 20s. After Dad left Santa Barbara, my spirit felt like an animal who had stepped in a trap and was bleeding, hurting and yelping. So I did what I had done when I was 25—I escaped to a faraway place: still limping, my spirit limb still attached.

I was thirty-two, just laid off from my job, and restless. And just like California had been, Italy was a place that offered a slew of distractions from my brokenness. My urge to get outta dodge for the sake of lost adventure—this was what the Cowboy had always done, too. Italy was my first time out of the country and I lived in Siena, in Tuscany, with a host family, and took Italian language lessons. Four grand and credit cards allowed me to experience Italy *humbly* for three months. I always chose experience and escape over financial responsibility, always with no regrets.

A new culture, a new challenge, a new love—an affair with my Italian language teacher—I felt alive like I hadn't since I'd moved to California. His name was Mauro and he was my Italian teacher, 17 years older than me—a former soccer player, speaker of four languages and a romantic who loved me and many others.

"Come si scrive?" (How do you write/spell that?) I incessantly asked. Even after weeks of lessons, I wouldn't speak Italian in class with my teachers and classmates. I was a perfectionist, pensive pupil who insisted on knowing how it was spelled before I would say it out loud. I sat quiet in class while the 19-year old American classmates sang their sentences, even after a night of drinking and smoking at the piazza. There were three Italian teachers –Sabrina, Elisa and Mauro; each one of them worked with me in different ways in attempt to break my silence. Sabrina and I went for walks, arm and arm, around the cobblestone streets of Siena, pointing out new vocabulary. The class went on daily excursions with the teachers and I observed Elisa converse with the advanced students— imperfect accents dictated the communication that I wanted to have and know. Mauro had a different approach all together, he used his Italian charm. As he led a lesson, writing a sentence on the board—his athletic build—broad shoulders and a soccer player's glutes, made me forget he was much older. His bottom lip was plump and looked more lick-able than the gelato Sabrina pointed out earlier that day. I bit my bottom lip trying to concentrate and read the sentence on the board. After a week of flirting with gelato, Mauro asked (in Italian) if I had plans for the weekend. "No, niente" I replied, my heart racing. "Would you like to spend the day with me bella?" and before I could stop myself, I finally found my Italian voice, "Si, come no" (Yes, how could I not?)

My interpretation of our first weekend together gave me a sense of belonging and comprehension of everything Italian. Mauro lived in a tiny village called Orgia; his villa was old and charming, but drafty. Night after night, the warmth of the fireplace coddled the villa and as we settled in for the night he placed the hot coals into an iron skillet to use in a bed-wagon frame or what the Italians call a *moine*. My Italian actually warmed the linens with the old-fashioned contraption. The bed stayed warm all night. In the morning I opened the shutters and peeked out the tiny window above the bed –I was living in Tuscany. Mauro had already gotten up, made a fire and espresso. "Buongiorno bella" he whispered as he wrapped his arms around my waist, pulled me to him and nibbled each lip individually and then together. In words and caresses, Mauro expressed his love of my body, especially next to his and we had sex for the second time that morning, this time in the kitchen. Still warm from his embrace, I drank the espresso and he started his day the same way he ended it—he took a shot of grappa and kissed my neck; I could feel the tingle of alcohol from his lips, cool my skin.

Daily life with Mauro warmed my Italian vocals like the coals heated the cold sheets every night. There was a second room in the petite villa, the door always closed. My Italian left for work and I stayed behind that afternoon to hang laundry, but my curiosity caught the cool draft coming from under the door. I peeked in and it seemed a room for storage, but I saw many women's belongings—shoes, dresses and pictures of a beautiful Spanish woman.

That night, after grappa, I asked my Italian about her. There were many like her—an opera singer from Germany, a striking blonde from London—and I was among them now, caught in this Italian lover cliché. Still, I was tempted to stay with him, hoping he would choose me and only me—living in his villa, making love every day, practicing my Italian. He was not *my* Italian; he was only my lover and my teacher. Despite exchanging a sincere, "Ti voglio bene" (I love you; I wish the best for you), I knew that it couldn't work. In just three short months in Italy I had adapted to the Italian "don't worry about it" mentality: the unfamiliar culture of Italy and the familiar unavailable love in Italy created just enough chaos that I was comfortable.

———◆———

I spent the Christmas after Dad died, house and cat sitting for my friend Barb in Santa Barbara. Her home—a quaint adobe with Zen landscaping and energy—seemed like a good place to convalesce. One of her cats –Alley, a polydactyl cat (has an extra toe on each front paw)—was shy, but always loved on me—I fit her attention criteria. I knew the cats well; I had answered a cat-sitting ad from Craigslist when I first moved to Santa Barbara. Barb and I had an instant connection and friendship—she was from Kansas and had also lived in Colorado. Barb was closer to my mom's age, but felt like an older sister and when I'd returned from Italy, with no money and no job, she invited me to stay with her for a few months. So here I was at her home while she was away for the holidays; I hadn't even pondered whether I would be alone or not—I didn't care enough to have that figured out.

Then Paolo, a dear Italian friend from Salsomaggiore, Italy phoned, "Ciao bella! Come va? I am here!" His voice and accent were a lovely distraction. Paolo had visited California before and made many friends—he insisted on spending Christmas with me and making authentic lasagna and tiramisu. We went to the grocery store –Paolo grabbing all he needed. "Don't you need cheese?" I asked. Paolo just laughed and shook his head and grabbed a stock of celery.

That afternoon, before his new California boyfriend would arrive to join us for dinner, I moped while Paolo cooked and ranted on and on about my needing to be happy and how he couldn't believe I didn't have cloth napkins to decorate the table. I was only housesitting *and* grieving—I had no idea where to find cloth napkins!

"Meleeesa! I cannot believe you have no napkins for beauty!"

I laughed. It felt good to laugh for a few seconds. (After looking everywhere, he insisted on asking Barb's neighbor.)

Earlier that day, my friend Chip, a photographer and traveler, had called to see how and what I was doing. I invited him to dinner; he took the train up from L.A. So there I sat, at a table set for a photo shoot, with three funny men—a photographer with great travel stories, an Italian and his lover— eating lasagna, drinking vino and conversing in mostly English. There was no Christmas tree, no Christmas music, no stockings, no turkey or apple pie— somehow, the absence of these holiday details was comforting, and distracted me momentarily from the fact that the Cowboy was gone. This was how I handled Christmas Day. Now how would I handle the rest of my life?

By New Years, I had had a fling with a newly separated politician—Republican, ugh, not my usual type—who drank himself into a happy manic rage and enjoyed gripping my little biceps with his bulked up hands. Bad romantic choices seemed to be a coping mechanism. My friends, who just wanted to say the right thing and offer condolences, would say, "Time heals", but I wondered if that were true. I resisted laughing or doing anything that felt good or promoted good health and healing. I promoted my own pain and suffering through not eating, not drinking enough water and not sleeping. I stared into the dark as I lay in bed, but I battled the urge to shut my eyes and sleep. After spending two weeks in the hospital with the Cowboy, with one eye open, waiting and needing to be present for a miracle or disaster, my body was trained not to fall asleep naturally.

I also struggled to get out a sentence to answer the common question asked with a tilted head: "How are you doing?" I winced and couldn't script a complete sentence; I often ended a thought or answer with "etc…" – "Oh thanks for checkin' in; I'm fine, ya know, just getting used to the idea, etc …" I knew what "etc…" meant; it meant accepting death and a permanent good-bye and I wasn't ready to acknowledge that just yet.

I made all of the rational and typical accommodations to deal with my grief—hospice grief meetings, therapy, and anxiety and depression medication. Sometimes the grief would lift, but it would be temporary. There was a 9-week grief workshop, meeting once a week for two hours—it was intense group therapy; still, I needed it two years in a row and even contemplated attending again. A discussion with my doctor about the loss and depression led us to a plan of medication for anxiety and depression for a year—that year quickly turned into three.

Three years after the Cowboy died, I decided to start classes in Alcohol and Drug Counseling (ADC) at Santa Barbara City College. By the time I registered, all of the ADC classes were full. All but one – *Family Dynamics*. Perfect. With my used textbooks in tow, I skipped down the stairs from the multi-level parking lot—it was too dark to see the water in the distance, but I breathed in the ocean air before I ran into the building, down the hall and into a small classroom, seats for about twenty. I didn't want to be late.

"According to therapist Anne Wilson Schaef, co-dependence is 'an addiction process lurking behind alcoholism'" the professor said, each hand in the front pockets of his jeans. He paced once as he paused so that all of us could think about what he had just said. I leaned forward in my desk and my eyes widened. I certainly was thinking about it and realized I was unconsciously shaking my head in agreement until a 20-something guy, with his bulky backpack, came rushing in sweaty and late.

Our professor, Gordon Coburn –everyone called him Gordy—handed out and read from the syllabus, "The Student Learning Outcomes of this class are:

1. Family Dynamics: Describe the dynamics of the chemically dependent family, including the survival roles.
2. Family Analysis: Describe and analyze personal family issues, roles and dynamics.
3. Therapeutics: Demonstrate effective therapeutic techniques for working with chemically dependent families."

I scanned through the timeline of my syllabus—week one, Family Therapy Theories; week two, The Family Disease; week three, The Family Roles and so on. This was the "tell me something I don't already know" stuff I had been searching for.

"Refer to page three of the syllabus. This explains a written assignment –30% of your grade that has been called the 'Hardest assignment of the entire ADC program'. It's an analysis of your own family system based on what you will learn in this course."

I couldn't wait for the next class.

For the next few months, every Monday night, I sat tall in my chair and looked straight ahead, raising my hand at every question or share. Gordy, in recovery for 25 years himself, stood at the front of the class as a professor and therapist—he had found healing and peace. I wondered what life would have been like if Dad had found recovery.

"According to John Bradshaw, shame is the base of all addiction—it's toxic shame. Bradshaw says, 'When we shame them, we are killing their souls,'" Gordy said and surveyed the faces of the classroom. I remembered Dad's "Anything" on his job applications—tears surfaced, and I looked down.

Later, I jumped in the discussion to ask, "So, being the family hero wreaks havoc on the codependent daughter—controlling, rescuing, following dysfunctional rules—but considering the bright side, is it naïve to think that it makes her stronger in a good way?"

In the conclusion of the final assignment, I wrote:

Much like a troubled child would create an imaginary friend to talk and play with, I survived my alcoholic family system by creating a personality and role that, I thought, protected me. I became a family hero and while it did save me in many ways by creating a bubble around the world I wanted to secure, it also caused stress and anxiety. Being a family hero made me feel like I was the parent and had to be in control; that was overwhelming and exhausting. I felt like I could not be vulnerable or even mess up in the slightest way.

Now, I have let go of the family hero persona a bit, but it is still there. The family hero role has brought me a long way in my life, much further than I thought in fact.

I am grateful that by instinct, I created a role that helped me survive the chaos among my family system. Ultimately it was the family hero role that wanted to get everything "perfect" even my healing as an adult child of an alcoholic, so I learned about and became aware of the disease and separating the disease from the person and that led to forgiveness, which has saved me. Thank you Family Hero for stepping in; I may not have gotten through my teen years without you.

At the end of the 10-page paper, Gordy wrote, among his encouraging notes, "I think you were also an unwilling Lost Child (withdrawn, needing solitude) when you stayed in your room and dreamed of creating a better life for yourself."

Twenty-Three

To have had a Cowboy Dad, like I did, is almost unheard of these days. Growing up on the ranch with tire swings, homemade tractor seats for Christmas, and merry-go-rounds. Witnessing Dad's work ethic, season after hard season. I've come to realize that most dads are not like this. My Dad the Cowboy inherited the disease of alcohol, which dented the essence of his character.

The effect of alcoholism sometimes disguises the true character of the person struggling with the addiction. Dad always wanted an association with "Rowdy" and the last few years of his life, that's what his friends and patrons of the Buckhorn Bar knew him as and there's no doubt he lived out that reputation.

Strangely, in no way do I associate Rowdy, my Cowboy Dad, with bad trouble, rather a good ole' cowboy just being himself and revealing a good-natured side even through his rowdiest and drunkest of days.

"Yip, yer dad and me were kicked out of his girlfriend's trailer for being too Rowdy. We'd been drinkin' again too much ya know and we just sat for hours on a street corner smokin and drinkin' and causin' a ruckus," Dad's buddy Dave shared with me at the hospital in Laramie.

I used to be ashamed of the one or two days he spent in jail or if I saw the Cowboy and he had a fat lip or black eye. Seriously? I thought. Or getting bucked off a horse and losing the ability to work for years because of a back injury—oh that's real responsible.

And as his daughter, I know there are stories that are not shared with me because they are the rowdiest of all; still, it's who he was—with and without alcohol. Dad was a Cowboy.

Rowdy, though, was a complex cowboy too. The rough and tough cowboy who burned bridges, stood up for his best bud in a bar brawl, and ultimately drank himself to death, was also the Cowboy who found his soul mate before he was twenty, the Cowboy who traded a pair of chaps for a kitten, practiced cheerleading with me and my best friend and gave me a pink feather for the cowboy hat I wouldn't have worn otherwise when I was six.

And rambunctious was often the Cowboy's most endearing trait—the rodeo, the free spirit, the wanderer—all contributed to the cowboy character that drew people near his smiling eyes, witty charm and kind heart. After one conversation with the Cowboy, you loved him and wanted to be around him, forgetting he passed out in the barn the day before.

I was thirty-four years old when the Cowboy died, and it was then that I realized I am a cowgirl. I can't saddle a horse, I've never competed in a rodeo and the last time I wore a cowboy hat, I was six. But the clothes don't make the cowboy or cowgirl—my dad gave up all of his cowboy belongings and his cowboy character remained true. Like my Dad, I lean toward the quiet solitude of the country and small town folks. I thrive in my free-spirit tendencies and soar in discovery and wandering, just like the Cowboy did. I never wanted or planned to be a cowgirl, but it started the day I

was born and the Cowboy held me. His cowboy gestures throughout my life and through his death have made a cowgirl out of me.

———◆———

S ometimes I speak about God like I still believe in Him. I don't
know if it's out of habit of being a strong believer for fifteen
years that I speak about Divine intervention or because I don't
know who or what else to give the credit to; I'm unsure about
many things now. The hopeful part of me thinks I might say these
things because my instinct is whispering to me, "God is still true."

I acknowledge the responsibility of owning one's life and when
I review my childhood and experiences with my Cowboy, I sepa-
rate my Dad from the disease. My faith has returned, but is still
unresolved, not because a higher power has acknowledged me in
the way I expected or desired, but because I don't feel hurt or sad
by memories of an alcoholic father.   Rather it is over-powered
by a huge aura of joy I have when I think of my hero and my role
model, in the most unsuspecting way—my Dad the Cowboy and
the childhood experiences he gave me on the ranch and in my life –
those memories feel like heaven to me. *That* is what reassures the
faith in my heart.

All these years I chased my Dad and I attempted to help and
ultimately save the Cowboy, but after he died I realized I was also
finding and understanding myself.

To protect against a broken heart, I even convinced myself that
I could handle it and after what we had been through, I was sure
that he would create his demise sooner than later. But as a higher
power would have it, I, the daughter, needed resolution and that
required more time, more understanding and forgiveness. The

Cowboy needed all of these things for himself as well before he could move on to a more peaceful place.

The Cowboy could have died of alcoholism soon after he departed from the bus station, but he didn't—he had more life to live and learn and I, his daughter, needed to come full circle to accept the situation, accept him for who he was and then I would be at peace and ready for my life. *At peace* meant more involved and more connected to him instead of less emotional or less attached; it meant being divinely prepared when he died. The concept of "ready" had to do more with a better understanding of myself—more attached and more in love with my Cowboy—caused by reconnection, conversations, memories and the death of my best friend Kiley. I needed to find forgiveness and resolution and love again, before Dad was ready to die. Dad died with me having a richer understanding of him, not an angry, regretful "you brought this upon yourself" perspective.

With the death of the Cowboy coming years later, I received grace through alcoholism. It takes significant loss to get to that level of appreciation, no matter how consciously grateful you are before the forever-gone reality settles in to your brain. Of course I would rather have them—Kiley and Dad—over the profound ah-ha, but this understanding is a crucial gift in healing and in living. In the beginning of my tragedy, I would not accept what was, but after three years of mourning, I started to accept my gift—the consequences of loss—which are intuition and insight for living and being.

The more willing I am to accept this conceptual gift, the more it continues to give; I don't just have acceptance—I *experience* acceptance. With a significant trauma comes a profound comprehension of the paramount level of gratitude toward what was lost. This is an earned prize; it's not a present I asked for or desire; in fact I didn't want it because if I accepted it, I accepted the loss. However, there's a turning point after the initial stages of grieving after the person is gone. Something in every day is a reminder that they are gone, but also that I am alive. So much of me is them— Kiley and Dad.

And now I experience my grief with grace; I feel the sadness *and* love with true acceptance, surreal understanding, rich reflection and awareness. I now function, conscious of these remarkable revelations *only* because my best friend and my dad passed away too soon. That was the heartbreak that pried open this place that I may have never journeyed through otherwise.

Twenty-Four

I was spring cleaning in December, which is entirely possible in California. A large, see-through plastic bin, containing paper work—taxes, medical records etc.—was sitting on my floor; it had been sitting in my closet for five years and I was moving it to storage. Standing across the room, I noticed an envelope with familiar handwriting addressed to me—Dad's handwriting!

It was as if the letter had been "hiding" until it was the right moment—it was the first time in three years since Dad's death that I was actually looking forward to the new year. It was as if the letter crawled out of a file and smooshed itself against the end of the clear box to shout "Look over here! Look at me—You're ready to read me!"

I looked at the letter inside the plastic bin and sang to myself, "It's another letter ... it's another letter." I had found other letters from my dad a year before; they were stashed away in an old desk. Sometimes his old letters were positive and sometimes they were written with a heavy sadness apparent in his words and shaky penmanship. I had gained more peace about my dad being gone and anything I could find or discover that was a part of him now brought joy, not pain.

I took the letter in both of my hands, holding it to my chest. My eyes filled with tears, but I was smiling. I examined every detail of the envelope—how he wrote my name and his return address

"Dad" with an address in Encampment, Wyoming. I was already in love with this letter.

Encampment? Huh. I could sense something special about this letter. Encampment was the small town near the Gingerquill Ranch where we lived in the cabin with the outhouse just before we moved to the Flying W Ranch. And then I noticed the date, stamped over the postage: June 26, 2006. This letter had been written shortly after I said good-bye to him at the Greyhound station; the day I said "I never want to see you again" and sent him on his way, not to see him again until November 2009, in that hospital in Wyoming.

Without realizing it, I'd carried heavy guilt about that day at the Greyhound bus station; the words spoken between me and the Cowboy and the years passed that we did not see each other—all of it lingered, and without a proper good-bye, finding peace had been nearly impossible. This guilt had hidden in my despair; I did not know I had been hauling it around until I read this letter again with a new perspective.

Melissa,

I finally took a day off and took the opportunity to write and catch up. I am getting a telephone in July. My ship has finally come in. I am writing again for the local newspaper and will continue submitting articles from time to time. I have got a great job managing a ranch east of Encampment. I will take over the cow herd ownership in 2 years. Then in exchange for running my cattle I will take care of the ranch. There will be about 200 head of mother cows. The owner is a professional barrel racer and the ranch has been in the family for over 100 years.

I finally took your advice and am making metal art again. I made another tree shovel and the owner asked me

what the hell I was doing ranching so I gave it to her. I also made her a metal stork for the flower garden. Right now I am working all of the time and I am doing home remodeling in my log home I get to live in. I am happier than I have been in a long time. I go to town 2 times a month for supplies etc. I am also learning how to cook better meals. I wish that I had paid more attention to your mother's cooking. Well, I love you and I hope you have some exciting news about your life. I will call when I get my phone in.
Love,
Dad

Had I read it any earlier, I would not have embraced the words as I did at that moment. Just reading, "Melissa" had me smiling and already crying as I anticipated the clues. The words were alive and spoke to me; they danced on the page, revealing his hope for himself. He'd found happiness in his life—fulfillment, even—doing everything he'd always loved.

I hadn't felt this much warmth in my heart since before he died. As I read the words, I remembered how I felt the first time I received the letter shortly after I said goodbye at the Greyhound station. I was still angry. I loved him, yes, but was still skeptical. This final letter shared with me what I had gathered and learned in the past three years since his death—that my hope in my Cowboy Dad was not superficial; it was alive and in his own words. He had never let alcoholism rob him of his aspirations for healing. The hope in this letter gave him the will to live and live he *did*, even as Rowdy, for another three years, which gave us the chance to reconnect through our phone calls.

And now, as I re-read each sentence, I saw that the Cowboy had returned home.

Twenty-Five

Dad called her "Ellie". She was a striking elk who showed up one spring in the midst of the cattle grazing in the pasture. The wild irises were abundant that May because of the snow melt. The stems were tall and the leaves like slender blades, sprouting velvety purple petals like antlers. Clusters of irises swayed and every so often I could see a rare white iris in the purple patches scattered throughout the pastures. Just like that rare white flower, Ellie, with her dainty, lady-like stance and brown-blonde hide, stood out among the stocky brown-black cattle. Ellie, the cattle, and the horses all grazed together.

Despite his natural instinct for being a hunter, the Cowboy instantly felt protective over the new visitor to the ranch and the herd. For a few years, Ellie pranced around gracefully with the herds as if she were their gracious queen, and in the snowy winters, she huddled with the cows to keep warm. The cows mooed and Ellie mooed. Ironically, female elk are actually called "cows", but dad couldn't quite figure out where she came from or why she wanted to graze and live among the lazy cattle. And every spring, I remember Ellie, the impersonator, standing in the corrals with the cattle, naively wanting to get branded with a "W" like the rest of the herd.

"Hayaw! Hayaw! Get outta there! Hayaw!" the Cowboy would rant towards Ellie to get her out of the shoots, a smile curling from his lips. Dad loved sharing stories of Ellie and he always looked after her. "She thinks she's a damn cow!" he would say, telling the story of how she followed the cattle into the shoot to get branded with the bright orange iron.

———————

Spring blew into summer and I would be a senior finally, but not before Dad would teach me to drag the fields.

"Climb on up-ere," he instructed as I stepped onto the machinery. It was an old, small red tractor. She was loud and I used all the strength of both arms to turn the wheel—no power steering.

"Go slow now … take wide turns, not too sharp, ya hear? The tires'll get tangled if ya do," he said. The Cowboy had attached old tires, linked with chains, shaped in a triangle, to the back of Red.

"Ya, I got it Pops." I shifted and bounced along, dragging the dried manure piles to disperse nutrients and keep the grass from being smothered. The first week, I got stuck and tangled up three times. Flustered, I stood tall on the tractor seat, waving my arms to get Dad's attention at the barn. He was patient, stopped what he was doing, and walked out to untangle the tire-drag mess.

"Guess I did a wide turn," I said, confused and a little embarrassed. Tough callouses were already cropping up on my fingers and hands.

He sensed defeat. "It's alright, you'll get it. Sometimes it's just the chains and tires and the groundrambunI get tangled up sometimes too." Dad fixed it and went back about his business in the barn.

Freckles appeared on my skin like the new grass would from the earth after dragging. Clear July skies gave way to thunderstorms and a light sprinkle to settle the dusty dried manure. The sun always peaked out again just before it left for the day, to return the next morning. And cattails grew along the ditches or near the ponds—their fluffy, white seeds floated through the air and along the surface of the water. Dad often brought a bouquet of cattails and irises to Mom.

Sometimes, after a long day, he'd take off his hat, and stand at the picture window. He'd spot Ellie among the cows in the pasture, and simply say, "I'll be damn."

-END-

Acknowledgments

Writing this book saved me. It was my biggest healer during a period of deep and seemingly endless grief. Reflecting, feeling, remembering, and writing this story created awareness and a deeper understanding of my dad's life as well as my own. This book has been my companion, and it is how I will introduce my dad, whom I love deeply, to people who never got to meet him. The retelling of this story came with many tears – happy and sad— but also with epiphanies and much clarity.

I have many dear people to thank who made this journey possible and who contributed to the unfolding of the Cowboy Dad story. I want to thank the friends who showed up in a multitude of small and meaningful ways—offering condolences; long, sad rides from the airport; and embraces when I awaited the inevitable, surreal news. During these days, my grief clouded my memory, but I remember the faces and presence of these dear friends. Trying to find the right words to share when someone is inconsolable can be daunting, but these dear ones *showed* me their love and concern through genuine friendship.

I would also like to thank some of the characters introduced in the book. The homeless man who stood outside of my workplace, holding his sign—I don't know who you are or where you are, but your presence stirred something in my heart to want to find and reconnect with my dad. The bartender at the Buckhorn Bar in Laramie Wyoming—I don't know your name, but I would know your voice if I heard it again. Thank you for allowing me to call my dad there to have conversations with him on the phone while he sat at the bar. And to the staff of doctors, therapists, and nurses in Laramie and especially Cheyenne, thank you so much for taking the extra time and effort with my Dad the Cowboy; it was such a beautiful scene to witness your care and thoughtfulness towards my dad. Dr. Tetenta, the cowboy would have been honored to meet the doctor who called him "The sickest man in Cheyenne" and humbled by your brilliance and contemplation of his dire needs.

To Kiley's family—my second family—her mom Ann, Lisa her sister, her husband Gibbs, and son and daughter, T.J. and Josie – you know what an impact Kiley had on my life as my best friend and I will forever hold our friendship close to my heart. She was an amazing woman and I am grateful that I get to see her through all of you. This is also a story of our unconditional friendship.

I'd like to thank my family, whom I dedicate this book to, my mom and my brother. Your experiences with the Cowboy inspired me to write this book. Mom, you were the parent who showed up in my life – graduations, travels, times of no work and uncertainty—you were always there. And R.J., through your life and hardships, we became closer, and not only are you the best little brother, but you are also a confidant. You remind me of all of the beautiful things about our dad, and I wouldn't have wanted to be with anyone else during those two weeks in Cheyenne; we held each other up. Mom and R.J., I cherish the time we had with our cowboy—on the ranch, but also in Cheyenne. Lastly, to Danny, my stepdad, you are part of this family. I have always felt that because of the way you love my mom, but also the way you show up in our lives—life occasions and hardships and even in Cheyenne.

Part of my healing process involved taking classes in alcohol and drug counseling. The knowledge I gained helped me understand myself, my family, my character, my tendencies, and the science of addiction. For the first time in my life, I actually understood what the hell was going on with my family and with my life. A special thank you goes to one of my professors, Gordy, at Santa Barbara City College, who shared his own story of recovery in class and inspired me with his perspectives on the disease of alcoholism. Gordy, you really shined a light on aspects of alcoholism that I didn't understand prior to your class. You are proof, along with other alcoholics in recovery that I have met, that one does not have to die from addiction and that there is hope.

Finally, I am indebted to my editor Kristen Keckler for her guidance and brilliant input and editing during this journey. I lived in Wyoming for a few months while I was finishing the book and my correspondence with her was something I looked forward to every day. Not only does she have the perfect credentials for my project (PhD in creative writing), but she is also a college professor of creative writing. So her edits came to me with a teacher's voice: insightful, with thoughtful instruction. Kristen, your humor (I still giggle when I think of dangling modifiers), encouragement, and writing notes about all of my "hot messes" have made my characters and scenes come alive. I felt like I had won the editor lottery. The way you helped me transform my story is something that I am so grateful for—you are my soulmate editor! The Cowboy would often say, "I'll be damn!" and you liked this expression in the book. I can't think of a better editor or person to which I would have wanted to share the *Cowboy Dad* expressions and story with, and I am humbled that you chose to edit, so attentively and sincerely, my story.

And last but not least, thank you to my Cowboy Dad, Randy.

Made in the USA
Columbia, SC
20 March 2021